UNDERSTANDING
ARTHUR MILLER

Understanding Contemporary American Literature
Matthew J. Bruccoli, General Editor

Volumes on

Edward Albee • John Barth • Donald Barthelme
The Beats • The Black Mountain Poets • Robert Bly
Raymond Carver • Chicano Literature
Contemporary American Drama
Contemporary American Horror Fiction
Contemporary American Science Fiction
James Dickey • E. L. Doctorow • John Gardner
George Garrett • John Hawkes • Joseph Heller
John Irving • Randall Jarrell • William Kennedy
Ursula K. Le Guin • Denise Levertov • Bernard Malamud
Carson McCullers • Arthur Miller • Toni Morrison's Fiction
Vladimir Nabokov • Joyce Carol Oates—Tim O'Brien
Flannery O'Connor • Cynthia Ozick • Walker Percy
Katherine Anne Porter • Thomas Pynchon • Theodore Roethke
Philip Roth • Mary Lee Settle • Isaac Bashevis Singer
Gary Snyder • William Stafford • Anne Tyler
Kurt Vonnegut • Tennessee Williams

UNDERSTANDING
Arthur
MILLER

ALICE GRIFFIN

UNIVERSITY OF SOUTH CAROLINA PRESS

Published in Columbia, South Carolina, by the
University of South Carolina Press

Manufactured in the United States of America

00 99 98 97 96   5 4 3 2 1

Grateful acknowledgment is given to Arthur Miller, Viking Pen-
guin, a division of Penguin Books USA INC., and Grove/Atlantic, Inc.,
for permission to quote from the following copyrighted works of Arthur
Miller: *After the Fall:* Copyright 1964 by Arthur Miller. *All My Sons:*
Copyright 1947, renewed 1975 by Arthur Miller. *The American Clock:*
Copyright 1982 by Arthur Miller. *Broken Glass:* Copyright 1994 by
Arthur Miller and Inge Morath. *The Crucible:* Copyright 1952, renewed
1980 by Arthur Miller. *Danger: Memory!* Copyright 1986 by Arthur
Miller. *Death of a Salesman:* Copyright 1949, renewed 1977 by Arthur
Miller. *Incident at Vichy:* Copyright 1964, 1965 by Arthur Miller. *The
Last Yankee:* Copyright 1993 by Arthur Miller and Inge Morath. *The
Price:* Copyright 1968 by Arthur Miller and Ingeborg M. Miller,
Trustee. *The Ride Down Mount Morgan:* Copyright 1991 by Arthur
Miller and Inge Morath Miller as Trustee. *Timebends:* Copyright 1987
by Arthur Miller. *A View from the Bridge* and *A Memory of Two
Mondays:* Copyright 1955, renewed 1983 by Arthur Miller. *A View from
the Bridge: A Play in Two Acts:* Copyright 1960, renewed 1983, 1985 by
Arthur Miller.

For John A. and John B.

CONTENTS

EDITOR'S PREFACE

The volumes of *Understanding Contemporary American Literature* have been planned as guides or companions for students as well as good nonacademic readers. The editor and publisher perceive a need for these volumes because much of the influential contemporary literature makes special demands. Uninitiated readers encounter difficulty in approaching works that depart from the traditional forms and techniques of prose and poetry. Literature relies on conventions, but the conventions keep evolving; new writers form their own conventions—which in time may become familiar. Put simply, *UCAL* provides instruction in how to read certain contemporary writers—identifying and explicating their material, themes, use of language, point of view, structures, symbolism, and responses to experience.

The word *understanding* in the titles was deliberately chosen. Many willing readers lack an adequate understanding of how contemporary literature works; that is, what the author is attempting to express and the means by which it is conveyed. Although the criticism and analysis in the series have been aimed at a level of general accessibility, these introductory volumes are meant to be applied in conjunction with the works they cover. They do not provide a substitute for the works and authors they introduce, but rather prepare the reader for more profitable literary experiences.

M. J. B.

PREFACE

At a recent London gathering of the British Universities Graduate Summer Program, foreign drama students, learning I was an American, were eager to discuss Arthur Miller, whose new play, *Broken Glass,* was opening at the Royal National Theatre. As they represented some thirty countries, I was pleased to learn that *Death of a Salesman* was being studied in China, that *The Crucible* was in the curriculum in Iceland, and that productions of Miller's works were staged regularly in Poland, the Czech Republic, and Italy as well as appearing in theater repertoires in France and Germany. A student from Japan was working on translations of the works into her native language.

The meeting confirmed what I already knew from my reading and travels: that the plays of Arthur Miller, so often considered a mirror of American life, touch and move audiences and readers throughout the world. Born in Manhattan, residing in a small town in Connecticut, Miller writes of familial love and its conflicts in terms that stir the minds and emotions of audiences not only in English-speaking nations but also in Brazil and Russia, Iceland and China. When Miller, directing *Death of a Salesman* in Beijing, explained to the Chinese actor of Biff the son's feelings of guilt and unrequited love for his father, the actor replied that he understood, because "it is very Chinese."

Like O'Neill, Miller always relates the family to a larger context, society and the world, his constant theme being "how may a man make of the outside world a home . . . to find the safety, the surroundings of love, the ease of soul, the sense of identity and honor which . . . [all] have connected in their memories with the idea of family?"

PREFACE

Despite moving some audiences to tears, Miller insists on making his readers and viewers think. He delights, as with *The Price,* in dialectical dialogue that forces the audience to come to its own conclusions: "I don't let you off the hook. . . . You want me to tell you what to think." He writes about "what is in the air," but the plays transcend the topicality that prompted them. Yet that topicality was only what some shortsighted reviewers saw when the plays first appeared.

I was fortunate to be a theater editor and critic as well as a university professor when the major plays opened and (with the exception of *Death of a Salesman*) received scant praise from the daily reviewers. It was the academic writers who, from the start, recognized the importance of Arthur Miller's plays. For all his international reputation, now secure, Mr. Miller has from the early days been most generous with his time to me and to others in academe, for which all of us are grateful.

In keeping with the editorial goals of this series, the major plays are discussed in depth, with analyses of characters, plot, themes, dramatic effects, and language, each work considered as an artistic entity, to which a chapter or half-chapter is devoted. One-acts of the 1980s, growing in popularity, are included, along with two of the later works, for which there exists little commentary. The two outstanding plays of the 1990s, *The Last Yankee* and *Broken Glass,* are discussed more fully. Because of the variety of printed texts of the plays, quotations are referred to by act and/or scene instead of by page numbers.

UNDERSTANDING
ARTHUR MILLER

CHAPTER ONE

Understanding Arthur Miller

Career

Arthur Asher Miller was born 17 October 1915 in New York City. His father, a Polish-Jewish immigrant, was a prosperous manufacturer of women's coats whose business failed when the market crashed in 1929. The family moved from a luxury apartment to a small house in Brooklyn, where Miller, as a student at Abraham Lincoln High School, was undistinguished in all but football. The Great Depression of the 1930s "was the ground upon which I learned to stand," says Miller.[1] Although jobs were virtually impossible to find in 1932, the year of "able-bodied men standing six and eight abreast along some warehouse wall waiting to be handed a bowl of soup or a piece of bread," he managed to be hired as a truck driver delivering auto parts for Sam Shapse, only to be fired when his business joined the "epidemic of rolling catastrophes that no one could stop."[2]

With so many seeking work, it was difficult for Miller to find another job, especially as most of the want ads specified "Gentile" or "Chr." Finding no such restrictions in an ad for a stockboy in an auto parts warehouse, Miller applied as one experienced with auto stock, but the firm did not respond. Shapse told Miller it was because he was Jewish, but, as most of the firm's customers were also Jewish, Shapse was determined to get Miller the job, which he did, Miller reported in a "Platform" talk at London's Royal National Theatre on 3 August 1994. To earn the five hundred dollars needed for his first year's tuition at the University of Michigan, Miller worked at the warehouse for two years. Although his high school grades were inadequate, he wrote to the university president asking for admission for one probationary year and was accepted. His nostalgic one-act play *A Memory of Two Mondays* is based upon his warehouse experiences: "All my work is autobiographical," Miller states in the Canadian television documentary in which he revisits his "home grounds" (24 October 1979).

In 1934 he enrolled at the University of Michigan, where two years later he entered a play contest, impelled more by the two hundred dollar prize than by ambition to become a dramatist. Having won the award, he enrolled in Professor Kenneth T. Rowe's playwriting class. The play, revised as *They Too Arise,* also won a Theatre Guild contest. Miller graduated in 1938 with a Bachelor of Arts degree in English and joined the Work Projects Administration's (WPA) Federal Theater Project in New York City. In order to be eligible, he had to prove that he was virtually penniless and living away from home with a boyhood friend, Sidney Franks. Sidney, a cum laude Columbia University graduate, had become a cop to support his father, a banker ruined by the Depression. Expecting the WPA investigator, Miller appeared at the small quarters to find Mr. Franks sitting in a worn armchair in "a furniture dump filled with eleven rooms' worth of stuff from their old apartment."[3] The characters and setting inspired *The Price.*

In 1940 Miller married his college sweetheart, Mary Grace Slattery, and they had two children, Robert and Jane. In World War II, when an old football injury made him ineligible for military service, he volunteered for shipbuilding work in the

UNDERSTANDING ARTHUR MILLER

Brooklyn Navy Yard. For the government he wrote radio scripts in support of the war effort and in 1943 was asked to write a screenplay based on Ernie Pyle's war reports. When Miller's script, giving equal importance to each man of the group, was rewritten to a Hollywood formula as *The Story of G.I. Joe,* he withdrew his name from the film credits. The interviews Miller had conducted with servicemen were published as reportage in 1944, however, in *Situation Normal:* "I tried to see a higher purpose operating among these men. . . . Though unable to define it in words, they shared a conviction that somehow decency was at stake in this grandest slaughter in history."[4] A second book was published the following year. The central character in the novel *Focus* is an anti-Semitic personnel director who prides himself on rejecting Jews who apply for jobs. When bad eyesight forces him to wear glasses, he suddenly looks Jewish and experiences the receiving end of anti-Semitism.

Miller's first Broadway play, *The Man Who Had All the Luck,* opened in 1944, only to close four days later. Looking back, Miller believes that the production was at fault, for the play is "a fable with no relation to realistic theatre, a fable . . . based on an obsessive grip of a single idea bordering on the supernatural," whereas the original production was "lit in reassuring pink and rose, a small-town genre comedy. Given the threatening elements in the story this atmosphere must indeed have been puzzling."[5] "The play was an investigation to discover what exact part a man played in his own fate," says Miller. David Beeves, a small-town businessman prospers, marries the girl he loves, and has a child, but he is "convinced that as his desires are gratified he is causing to accumulate around his own head an invisible but nearly palpable fund, so to speak, of retribution. . . . The play is built around his conviction of impending disaster," which never occurs, even though "he tries to bring it on in order to survive it and find peace."[6] His brother is the favored son, to whose training as a baseball pitcher their father had in vain devoted his entire attention. In writing of the father and his two sons, Miller notes, "the crux of *All My Sons* . . . was formed; and the roots of *Death of a Salesman* were sprouted."[7]

When *All My Sons* opened on Broadway in 1947 its warm reception immediately conferred fame upon the young playwright, hailed as everything from "promising" to "magnificent." The plot suggested itself to Miller when his mother-in-law happened to mention a young girl in Ohio who had turned her father in to the authorities for selling defective parts in wartime to the armed forces. Unprepared for instant success and unaccustomed to unsought attention, Miller took refuge in a a factory job, "as though to insure my continuity with the past," and worked for forty cents an hour assembling wooden box dividers for beer bottles. He was attempting, he says, "to be part of a community" instead of accepting the isolation that fame brought. "But I was also reacting to my having excelled, and the contradictions of the old fraternal competition flamed up. . . . I wanted and did not want to excel over my brother."[8] His older and more handsome brother, Kermit, he characterizes as being the steadier and more responsible of the two as children, while, as the younger, Miller recalls, he demanded instant gratification. In *Timebends* Miller details the ongoing competition between the brothers, their actual childhood fights, which would continue for many years, combined with his "secret vision" of pushing his brother "beyond reach of effective action" in conflicts that were resolved "on a third plane, the plane of art."[9]

Produced in 1949, *Death of a Salesman,* Miller's third father-and-sons work, was acclaimed by the critics and won a Pulitzer Prize as well as a Drama Critics' Circle award. It is Miller's most famous play and has been produced all over the world. *Salesman in Beijing* (1984), the playwright's account of its impact in China, where the profession of salesman is unknown, testifies to the universality of the play's theme and characters.

As the 1950s began, *Death of a Salesman* attracted controversy that had nothing to do with its artistic merit. The American Legion protested the movie version in some cities and in others closed the touring stage production by boycotting it as an "un-American" attack on capitalism. Fearful of losing revenue, the film studio decided to precede the movie with a short film praising the occupation of salesman and canceled it only when Miller threatened to withdraw the movie. The attack on *Death of a Salesman* characterized the anticommunist movement known as McCarthyism.

Senator Joseph McCarthy's power was based on a theory that communists in government positions, the military, and the arts were threatening the American way of life. "Once it was conceded that absolutely any idea remotely similar to a Marxist position was not only politically but morally illicit, the liberal . . . was effectively paralyzed," notes Miller.[10] Miller saw actors, writers, and directors called before McCarthy's investigating committee to confess to socialist principles and to name others who shared these sympathies. If they did so in public, they would be "cleansed" and allowed to continue their careers; if they refused, they would be deprived of their livelihoods by their employers, including the film and radio-television studios, theater producers, and publishers.

Two leading actors, Fredric March and his wife, Florence Eldridge, having been named as communists, were suing their accuser for libel; deprived of film roles until they "cleared" their names, they decided to appear on Broadway in a play by Henrik Ibsen, *An Enemy of the People,* in which the idealistic hero's situation resembled theirs—accused by mob hysteria of threatening the well-being of the home town. When Miller was asked to write the adaptation, based on a literal translation of the play, he readily accepted, believing it applied "to our moment in America— the need, if not the holy right, to resist the pressure to conform."[11] The dialogue is sinewy and forthright, and the version has proved popular in regional productions, though it was a financial failure on Broadway in 1950. In addition to the timely theme of Ibsen's play, Miller no doubt was attracted by its conflict between the two Stockmann brothers, one a doctor (played by March), whose discovery that the town's hot springs, thought to be healthful, are actually poisonous, and the other the town mayor, who, along with the townspeople, insists upon suppressing the discovery, for they see in it the destruction of the town's prosperous tourist economy.

Quite by accident, a copy of Marion Starkey's book on the Salem witch trials, *The Devil in Massachusetts,* came to Miller's notice. The analogy to the hearings in Washington was clear: they were "avowedly ritualistic" and insisted on "public confession" by which "*moral* guilt . . . could easily be made to disappear by ritual speech: intoning names of fellow sinners and recanting former beliefs."[12] When *The Crucible* appeared on Broadway in 1953, it was attacked for its parallels to the Senate "witch hunts" and was not even judged a good play by the reviewers; later critics were to proclaim it "great." It is Miller's most widely produced work, although he reflects that in some instances merit may not be the main reason for its popularity in American schools: "Teachers feel protected by the play because they are being attacked for teaching immoral or anti-social things by some narrow-minded people."[13]

By 1956 Miller was well-known for his crusading spirit and his fearless defense of freedom of expression. When he applied for a routine renewal of his passport, the House Un-American Activities Committee seized the opportunity to summon Miller to a hearing. Nor were they unaware of the publicity to be gained, for Miller by then not only was a famous playwright but also was married to film star Marilyn Monroe. Sounding like John Proctor in *The Crucible,* Miller refused to name others (already known to the committee) as communists or communist sympathizers: "I want you to understand that I am not protecting the Communists or the Communist Party. I am trying to and I will protect my sense of myself. I could not use the name of another person and bring trouble on him. . . . I take the responsibility for everything I have ever done, but I cannot take responsibility for another human being."[14] He was cited for contempt, fined, and given a thirty-day suspended jail sentence. He appealed and two years later won his case.

Miller wonders in his autobiography, *Timebends,* whether his past espousals of liberal causes might not have been more moral than political: "a moral act of solidarity with all those who had failed in life . . . a redemption from the self." He compares it to his taking the factory job after the success of *All My Sons,* but recognizes that by 1956 "I had learned to trace the leveling impulse to less exalted arenas than morality and public reform, back to the ancient competitions with my brother and illiterate father, whose metaphoric retaliation for my victories I had dodged by declaring my equality with the least of the citizenry while in the real world working day and night to achieve what glory and superiority my art might win me."[15]

In Hollywood briefly in 1950 with his unproduced movie script about racketeers and the longshoremen's union, Miller had met Marilyn Monroe, and the two had fallen in love. Emotionally fragile, she sought in the tall, rangy playwright, whom she compared to Lincoln, the strength to face a world she viewed as hostile. They married in 1956, after his divorce from his first wife. Miller writes of Monroe with compassion in *Timebends,* relating the joys and anguish of their union. During that time he produced no plays but, instead, devoted three years to writing a movie for her, *The Misfits,* based on his short story of the same name. By the time the film was released in 1961 they had been divorced. The following year Miller married Inge Morath, an Austrian professional photographer. Happily married ever since, they have collaborated on three books, *In Russia* (1969), *In the Country* (1977), and *Chinese Encounters* (1979), with text by Miller and photographs by Morath. They have a daughter, Rebecca. Asked by a group of Broadway actors in 1955 for a work they could present on Sundays, when their theater was closed, Miller wrote *A View from the Bridge.* The story of an obsessed longshoreman, presented in the powerful, unadorned mode of Greek tragedy, it is often revived, most recently in London's West End in 1995, following an extensive tour.

In 1964, after Miller's nine-year absence from Broadway, *After the Fall* opened, followed later in the year by *Incident at Vichy*. Both were written for the acting company of the new Lincoln Center Theater, a promising venture that foundered. Although Miller is rarely favored by a majority of the New York reviewers, he was not prepared for their vilification of *After the Fall*, in which the character Maggie resembles Marilyn Monroe. Faring better with the critics was *Incident at Vichy*, a taut yet philosophical treatment of guilt versus responsibility.

Four years later praise was all but unanimous for *The Price,* which treats hostility between competitive brothers, a favorite subject of Miller's. It seemed inevitable that next he would tackle the source, the biblical story of Cain and Abel. Discussing *The Creation of the World and Other Business* in 1972, Miller told Josh Greenfeld, "my plays are getting more and more mythological." In *Creation,* he explained, the characters are "actually mythological. . . . And perhaps it isn't as obvious to others as it is to me that the characters in all my other plays are also mythological. . . . I don't think I can write until I see some mythos." He explained that earlier "the individual overwhelms your vision. But then when you see three, five, thirty variations of the individual, there seems to be an archetype lurking in the background."[16]

The play's combination of styles confused the reviewers: the treatment of God and Lucifer and Adam and Eve is at times poetic, at others folksy. In the final sequences between Cain and

Abel, however, the play gains strength and momentum to arrive at a powerful conclusion. An unrepentant Cain, having killed Abel, challenges God: "When God repents His injustice, I will repent my own!" Disappointed in the family, God tells them: "You are all worthless! The mother blames God, the father blames no one, and the son knows no blame at all." The play is seldom revived, although it was performed in a musical version at the University of Michigan in 1974.

In 1980 Miller's film adaptation of Fania Fenelon's book *Playing for Time* was hailed as one of television's all-time best serious dramas. Vanessa Redgrave impressively portrayed the sensitive half-Jewish singer Fania sent to the Nazi concentration camp at Auschwitz, where through determination she survives its horrors: "I've always had to have an aim in life—something I wanted to do next. That's what we need now if we're ever to get out of here alive." A stage version was produced in 1985 and published in 1990.

In the 1980s *The American Clock* and *The Archbishop's Ceiling* (written earlier) were presented on the British stage in productions Miller regarded as definitive and on which he based the revisions published in 1983 and 1984, respectively. The latter drew from Miller's experiences with writers in the Soviet bloc whom he met when serving as president of PEN, the international writers' association advocating freedom of expression. Four new one-act plays were produced in two programs, *Two-Way Mirror* (*Elegy for a Lady* and *Some Kind of Love Story*) in 1982 and in 1987 *Danger: Memory!*, consisting of *I Can't Remember Anything* and *Clara.* Miller's excellent autobiography, *Timebends,* appeared as a Book-of-the-Month Club popular selection in 1987.

UNDERSTANDING ARTHUR MILLER

While Miller is appreciated in the United States, he is revered in England, where his works thrive in the noncommercial atmosphere of the Royal National, Royal Shakespeare, and Young Vic companies, in productions with leading, classically trained actors. Celebrating his seventieth year, the University of East Anglia named its center for American studies the Arthur Miller Centre, and in 1987 the British Broadcasting Corporation (BBC) presented on radio his early poetic historical drama, *The Golden Years.* Written in 1940, it deals with the conquest of unresisting Montezuma and his kingdom by Cortez and a handful of Spaniards. Miller chose England for the 1991 premiere of *The Ride Down Mt. Morgan,* set in America in the 1980s, about a man who has everything, almost.

By the mid-1990s, approaching his eightieth year, Miller had revised *The Crucible* for an important film version and produced two more major plays, *The Last Yankee* (1992) and *Broken Glass* (1994). Both works were praised by British theater critics, with the *Financial Times* of 27 January 1993 proclaiming of *Yankee,* "You will seldom see anything better on the stage," and the London *Sunday Times* of 14 August 1994 declaring *Broken Glass* "one of the great creations of the American theatre."

Art and Dramatic Theory

Arthur Miller's extensive articles, essays, speeches, and introductions provide a key to understanding his aims and appreciating his art. From the fifty-two-page introduction to his *Collected Plays,* which appeared in 1957, to the 1993 essay "About Theater Language," Miller's theater essays are considered major contributions to modern dramatic theory.[17] Miller discusses not only the aesthetics of his plays but also what was "in the air," surrounding and prompting their composition: the artistic, commercial, political, and social climates of the times.

Miller acknowledges his debt to Ibsen in *All My Sons*. He admires Ibsen's "ability to forge a play upon a factual bedrock. A situation in his plays is never stated but revealed in terms of hard actions, irrevocable deeds; and sentiment is never confused with the action it conceals."[18] Miller also appreciates Ibsen's solution to the "biggest single dramatic problem, namely, how to dramatize what has gone before," to achieve "a viable unveiling of the contrast between past and present, and an awareness of the process by which the present has become what it is. . . . What is precious in the Ibsen method is its insistence upon valid causation."[19] One might apply to Miller's own plays his observations on Ibsen's.

Miller also notes that "for younger writers such as myself, [Clifford] Odets for a couple of years was the trailblazer. . . . he had dared to invent an often wildly stylized stage speech. . . . It was as though Odets were trying to turn dialogue into jazz. . . . It was an invented diction of a kind never heard before on stage— or off."[20] Miller astutely observes that Odets's dialogue was not realistic but poetic. Likewise, although Miller's dialogue often has been praised for its realism, it is carefully crafted to fit his characters. His best lines have become familiar and oft-used quotations not because they sound like everyday speech but because they are "poetic realism": "Attention must be paid." "He's liked, but he's not—well liked" (*Death of a Salesman*); "Is the accuser always holy now?" (*The Crucible*); "I never saw you as a man. I saw you as my father" (*All My Sons*); and "It's not your guilt I want, it's your responsibility" (*Incident at Vichy*).

"My own tendency," writes Miller, "has been to shift styles according to the nature of my subject . . . in order to find speech that springs naturally out of the characters and their backgrounds rather than imposing a general style."[21] He points out that the New Englanders in *The Last Yankee* do not speak like the working men and women in *A Memory of Two Mondays* or Eddie Carbone and his fellow longshoremen in *A View from the Bridge*. For *The Crucible* he invented a language that began with the syntax and idiom of the verbatim court records of the period and proceeded to take on flavor and a poetry of its own which is stark, strong, and earthy, like the people who spoke it.

"Idea is very important to me as a dramatist," says Miller, noting that playwrights need not have invented new or original ideas, but, rather, "they have enunciated not-yet-popular ideas which are already in the air, for which there has already been a preparation. . . . Which is to say that once an idea is 'in the air' it is no longer an idea but a feeling, a sensation, an emotion, and with these the drama can deal."[22] Miller may draw his theme from ideas "in the air," but his plots often are suggested by actual events he hears about. A casual remark by his mother-in-law was the impetus for *All My Sons*. The story of *A View from the Bridge* was told by a friend to Miller long before he began the play. *Incident at Vichy* was prompted by the experiences of a psychiatrist acquaintance apprehended by the Nazis.

Images drawn from life, sometimes his own, may converge to suggest a play: *Broken Glass* is based on the picture of a woman he knew in the 1930s who inexplicably lost the use of her legs;

Death of a Salesman, he says, began as a series of images evoking the theme of *ubi sunt:* the little frame house, now deserted, which once rang with children's voices and the chamois cloth, now lost, once used to proudly polish the car on a Sunday afternoon. Miller admits that his plays contain elements that are autobiographical: his boyhood friend Sidney who became a cop to support his Depression-ruined father suggested Victor in *The Price;* his cousin Abby, Happy in *Death of a Salesman.* One suspects that the mother of young Lee, so warmly and sympathetically depicted in *The American Clock,* and Quentin's mother, unconsciously cruel to both husband and son in *After the Fall,* resemble in part Miller's own mother, who, like Sylvia in *Broken Glass,* felt she threw her life away when she married, as reported in his autobiography. His illiterate father, says Miller, was a helpful testing ground for the plots of his plays: "He'd ask what I was writing, and I'd tell him the story. I could see in his eyes whether it was going to hit home. I can't remember a time when he was wrong. . . . He wanted to be astonished, and when he was—Boy, the power that came out of him."[23]

Although some of his characters may be suggested by his own life and experience, Miller insists that they are dramatic entities, created for the stage and existing only in their life there. With no play was this more ignored than *After the Fall.* Only in recent years could commentators evaluate this work on its own merits without analyzing Maggie as Marilyn Monroe and Quentin as Miller and accusing him of staging his own life. More often the reverse seems to be true: the viewers or readers recognize themselves or their parents or friends in the plays, for one of Miller's strongest gifts is to create unforgettable individuals who also are universal: Willy Loman is the best example, but Linda

UNDERSTANDING ARTHUR MILLER

Loman, Joe Keller, John Proctor, Eddie Carbone, and Sylvia Gellberg share this distinction. Often overlooked is Miller's talent for revealing the complexities and conflicts of his individual characters within a group situation, be it family or friends or politics or business, set within the larger environment of society itself.

When Miller began his career, he found in Eugene O'Neill a writer who, like himself, was unafraid of expressing ideas: "If he glimpsed any salvation, it was . . . in the tragic cleansing of the life-lie permanently ensconced in the human condition. Since [unlike Odets] he took no responsibility in theory for a new and better policy to take the place of the corrupted present one, he was free to explore all sorts of theatrical means by which to set forth the situation of the damned. . . . he was hunting the sounding whale of ultimate meaning."[24] From *The Man Who Had All the Luck* to *The Last Yankee* Miller attacks "the evaluation of people by their success or failure" and denies "the efficacy of property as a shield against psychological catastrophe."[25] The theme does not endear him, any more than it did O'Neill, to many who hold sacred the views these playwrights question. A favorite Miller theme treats the need to face reality rather than to cling to illusion, as demonstrated in *Death of a Salesman.*

In *Death of a Salesman,* Miller says, he "aimed to make a play with the veritable countenance of life. To make one the many, as in life, so that 'society' is a power and a mystery of custom and inside the man and surrounding him, as the fish is in the sea and the sea inside the fish, his birthplace and burial ground, promise and threat."[26] Miller often uses the fish-water analogy to explain that a serious treatment of a human being must encompass the society that surrounds him or her as the force that has conditioned thoughts, culture, attitudes, and values. Another axis is the family, as in Miller's constant theme that encompasses the individual, society, and the family: "How may a man make of the outside world a home? How and in what ways must he struggle, what must he strive to change and overcome within himself and outside himself if he is to find the safety, the surroundings of love, the ease of soul, the sense of identity and honor which, evidently, all men have connected in their memories with the idea of family?"[27]

The theme of responsibility for one's actions, not only to one's family but also to the larger world, first appears in *All My Sons.* It can be seen as well in Miller's adaptation of Ibsen's *An Enemy of the People* and in *A View from the Bridge.* That one must accept in the present the consequences of one's actions in the past is a related theme, which he explores in *The Price.* To Miller, assuming responsibility also means that guilt is not enough; one must acknowledge responsibility for evil in the world, even for so horrendous an aberration as the Holocaust, as he points out in *After the Fall* and *Incident at Vichy.* Blaming other people, or circumstances, for one's own failures is a form of denial, of evading responsibility, which Miller exposes in *The Price.* Unlike O'Neill, whose characters in *Long Day's Journey into Night* seek to assign blame rather than to accept responsibility, Miller still sees hope, still remains optimistic. Just as Quentin in *After the Fall* must take up the idiot child that is his life and embrace it with love, so Patricia in *The Last Yankee,* to lift her depression, must accept Leroy's advice: "you just have to love this world."

Miller's plays attempt neither "escape from process and determinism" nor "inverted romanticism" but, instead, seek a new balance that "embraces both determinism and the paradox of will." "If there is one unseen goal" toward which his plays strive, he says, "it is that very discovery and its proof—that we are made and yet are more than what made us."[28]

Notes

1. Arthur Miller, "The Shadows of the Gods," in *The Theater Essays of Arthur Miller,* ed. Robert A. Martin (New York: Viking Press, 1978), 176.

2. Arthur Miller, *Timebends* (New York: Grove Press, 1987), 214. Most of the biographical details in this chapter are from this source.

3. Ibid., 245–47.

4. Ibid., 277.

5. Arthur Miller, "Introduction," *The Golden Years* and *The Man Who Had All the Luck* (London: Methuen Drama, 1989), 6.

6. Miller, "Introduction to the *Collected Plays*," *Theater Essays,* 125.

7. Ibid., 126.

8. Miller, *Timebends,* 276.

9. Ibid., 47, 145–46.

10. Ibid., 341.

11. Ibid., 324.

12. Ibid., 331.

13. Heather Neill, "Leading Role," *Times Educational Supplement*, 9 September 1994, 15.

14. House Committee on Un-American Activities, "Testimony of Arthur Miller, accompanied by Counsel, Joseph L.

Rauh, Jr.," *Investigation of the Unauthorized Use of United States Passports,* 84th Congress, pt. 4: 4684–90.

15. Miller, *Timebends,* 395.

16. Josh Greenfeld, "'Writing Plays Is Absolutely Senseless,' Arthur Miller Says, 'But I Love It. I Just Love It,'" *New York Times Magazine,* 13 February 1972, 37.

17. Arthur Miller,"Introduction," *Collected Plays* (New York: Viking Press, 1957), 3–55; "About Theater Language," *The Last Yankee* (New York: Penguin Books, 1993), 75–98. The earlier major essays, including the 1957 "Introduction," appear in *Theater Essays.*

18. Miller, "Introduction to the *Collected Plays*," *Theater Essays,* 131.

19. Ibid., 133.

20. Miller, "About Theater Language," 83–84.

21. Ibid., 91–92.

22. Miller, "Introduction to the *Collected Plays*," *Theater Essays,* 119, 122.

23. "Miller's Tales," The Talk of the Town, *New Yorker,* 5 April 1994, n.p.

24. Miller, "About Theater Language," 79–80.

25. Arthur Miller, "Introduction," *The Man Who Had All the Luck,* 6.

26. Miller, "Introduction to the *Collected Plays*," *Theater Essays,* 143.

27. Arthur Miller, "The Family in Modern Drama," *Theater Essays,* 73.

28. Miller, "Introduction to the *Collected Plays*," *Theater Essays,* 170.

CHAPTER TWO

All My Sons

The trouble with Joe Keller in *All My Sons,* says Arthur Miller, "is not that he cannot tell right from wrong but that his cast of mind cannot admit that he, personally, has any viable connection with his world, his universe, or his society." The play addresses the question of relatedness, "of a moral world's being such because men cannot walk away from certain of their deeds."[1] The playwright notes that the story was told him by "a pious lady from the Middle West" about a neighborhood family that "had been destroyed when the daughter turned the father in to the authorities on discovering that he had been selling faulty machinery to the Army" during World War II.[2] Second of Arthur Miller's father-and-sons trilogy, *All My Sons* was preceded by *The Man Who Had All the Luck* and followed by *Death of a Salesman.*

The action begins on a placid Sunday morning in August, two years after the war ended. Father Joe, now a prosperous appliance manufacturer, supplied parts to the army during the war. Son Chris has joined the business, having returned home after wartime service. During the war his brother Larry, a pilot, was reported missing in action. Neighbors drop by to greet Larry's former fiancée, Ann, who has arrived for a visit. Chris hopes to marry her, but they are cautious about informing his mother, Kate. She refuses to believe that Larry is dead and regards as an omen the fact that the memorial tree they planted, "too soon" she asserts, has blown down the night before.

UNDERSTANDING ARTHUR MILLER

In defending the criticized pace of the first act, Miller explains that "it was designed to be slow. . . . so that when the first intimation of the crime is dropped a genuine horror might begin to move into the heart of the audience, a horror born of the contrast between the placidity of the civilization on view and the threat to it that a rage of conscience could create."[3] Miller acknowleges Ibsen's influence on *All My Sons;* like Ibsen, Miller brings "the past into the present . . . because its theme is the question of actions and consequences, and a way had to be found to throw a long line into the past in order to make that kind of connection viable."[4]

As act 1 unfolds, details of the past emerge: amiable Joe Keller had been jailed, along with his partner, Ann's father, for shipping the army defective parts, resulting in the deaths of twenty-one pilots. His partner is still in jail, but on appeal Joe was exonerated and released, for he was ill at home the day the cylinder heads were shipped. Neither Ann nor her brother George has forgiven their father, though Joe pleads to Ann on his behalf. Good-natured, joking, uneducated, but with "a peasant-like common sense," Joe has regained the goodwill of neighbors previously outraged. Yet Kate's anxiety, unexplained illness, superstition, and denial of Larry's death suggest that she, like Joe, is self-deceived in believing that all is well. By the end of the act their uneasiness implies guilt, when they overhear Ann's telephone conversation and learn that her brother George, now a lawyer, is on his way to see them. "Be smart now, Joe," cautions Kate. "The boy is coming. Be smart." Keller, so self-assured earlier, now "in hopeless fury" goes into the house and slams the screen door violently. The sound is symbolic, upsetting the tranquillity of the surroundings and of the family.

ALL MY SONS

Self-made Joe, devoted Kate, and loving Chris at first appear to be an ideal family. As the play develops, their self-deception and guilt are laid bare, as each reacts to the crisis that arises "whenever the hand of the distant past reaches out of its grave . . . to reveal some unreadable hidden order behind the amoral chaos of events." "That emergence," says Miller, "is the point of *All My Sons*—that there are times when things do indeed cohere."[5]

Joe is convincingly drawn as a father whose boundaries are determined by the family; everything he does is motivated by a commendable concern for them and their welfare. But he is self-deceived in his isolation, of which the hedged-in backyard is symbolic. Son Chris has wider horizons; the conviction of responsibility for others is born of his war experience. Chris feels guilty for returning alive when so many of the men under his command had been killed. He explains to Ann in act 1 why he seems distant and "ashamed": "They didn't die; they killed themselves for each other. . . . a little more selfish and they'd've been here today. . . . Everything was being destroyed, see, but it seemed to me that one new thing was made. A kind of . . . responsibility. Man for man."[6] He confesses to her his surprise on returning home and finding "nobody was changed at all. It seemed to make suckers out of a lot of guys. I felt wrong to be alive."

When Ann responds that he should be proud that his father "put hundreds of planes in the air" for the war effort, Chris asserts, "I'm going to make a fortune for you!" His ambivalence in criticizing war profiteers while accepting the profits has led some commentators to question Chris's idealism. But those with battlefield experience of World War II praise the playwright's perception when Chris relates (to use Miller's words in *Situation Normal* [1944]) "that one-time feeling of exhiliration" at "helping an enormous mass of men toward a great and worthy goal."[7] To return after that experience and find, as Chris says, "there was no meaning in it here; the whole thing to them was a kind of a—bus accident," would explain his ambivalence, confusion, and guilt.

To Joe's warning in act 1 that Kate will never agree to Chris's marrying his brother's fiancée, Chris replies that he will marry her and move away. "You've got a business here," Keller reminds him. As he pressures his father to approve the marriage, Chris echoes Joe's own sentiments: "If I have to grub for money all day long at least at evening I want it beautiful. I want a family, I want some kids. I want to build something I can give myself to. Annie is in the middle of that. Now . . . where do I find it?"

It is apparent that Larry was the favored son, much as Miller in *Timebends* portrays his brother Kermit, who served in World War II, while his younger brother was rejected for military service. Miller's *Situation Normal* is dedicated to "Lieutenant Kermit Miller," who, unlike Larry, returned safely. Kate's devotion and her opposition to Chris's marriage to Ann—which would confirm Larry's death—reflect the mother's subliminal resentment that Chris was the brother who returned alive. In act 1, as he responds to his father's reprimand that Ann is "Larry's girl," Chris complains that he has always played second fiddle: "Every time I reach out for something I want, I have to pull back because other people will suffer. My whole bloody life, time after time after time." As the disregarded son who yearns for recognition, Chris might well go to the extremes of idealism which neighbor Sue pictures as "living next door to the Holy Family."

ALL MY SONS

Psychiatrist Daniel E. Schneider sees Chris as "an unpreferred son forced . . . to a subsidiary position in the affections of his father and mother, and even of the heroine . . . since she was betrothed to the preferred son." Schneider believes that through the "power of the playwright," Chris's inner hate and vengeance are transformed into "logical and rational justification for all his goals"—winning Ann, crushing his mother's fantasy that Larry lives, and the "annihilation of the father."[8] At the beginning of act 3, after Chris has learned the truth and rushed away, Joe finds solace in contrasting him to Larry: "Goddam, if Larry was alive he wouldn't act like this. He understood the way the world is made. He listened to me. To him the world had a forty-foot front, it ended at the building line." Chris, he says, "don't understand money. Too easy, it came too easy. Yes, sir. Larry. That was a boy we lost. Larry. Larry."

Miller notes that in his first version of the play, originally titled *The Sign of the Archer:* "Kate Keller was in a dominating position; more precisely, her astrological beliefs were given greater prominence. . . . Where in previous plays I might well have been satisfied to create only an astrologically obsessed woman, the obsession now had to be opened up to reveal its core of self-interest and intention on the character's part."[9] While Joe's camaraderie and Chris's idealism might be considered extreme, Kate's "core of self-interest" is at the root of her denial of Larry's death. As she shares the guilty secret of Joe's responsibility for the death-dealing cylinder heads, she suffers from the even more horrifying knowledge that, if Larry is dead, then Joe may have killed him. Ann's marriage to Chris, which Kate opposes, would confirm Larry's death.

Criticized as too convenient a plot device is Kate's slip of the tongue at the end of act 2, when she brags that Joe "hasn't been laid up in fifteen years." Thus, his "flu" on the day of the fatal shipment was a convenient alibi, and both George and Chris are now convinced of Joe's complicity. Possibly, Kate blurts out the truth because the burden of guilt is finally too much for her. Christopher Bigsby notes that "Chris's mother plays her final card in order to prevent the marriage which will signal the end of her hope. She reveals her husband's guilt to her son."[10] Certainly, the character of Kate has more complexity than Benjamin Nelson finds: "the problem of Kate's obsessive delusions about her dead son . . . is resolved so rapidly and neatly that one cannot help but suspect the depth of her original dilemma."[11]

Miller reports that when *All My Sons* was presented in Israel in 1977 it "was centered on Kate, the mother, which was an emphasis our original production had bypassed in favor of the father-son conflict." A London production also centered upon Kate. Miller wonders whether it was "a certain ambiguity in Kate" which had confused critic Ward Morehouse, who at the first production asked Miller, "What's it about?" "For while trying to put it out of her mind," the playwright continues, "she knows from the outset that her husband indeed shipped faulty plane engine elements. . . . Her guilty knowledge [is] obdurately and menacingly supressed."[12]

In reacting to their guilty secret, Joe and Kate are as unlike each other as Macbeth and Lady Macbeth. Joe believes he can "walk away" from his deed and retreat into "the fortress of unrelatedness." But, says Miller, "the structure of the play is designed to bring [him] into the direct path of the consequences he has wrought."[13] Joe will learn the lesson that so many of

ALL MY SONS

Miller's heroes and heroines must learn: to assume responsibility for one's own actions and to face the consequences. Early in the play Chris observes that Joe has "a talent for ignoring things," to which his father replies, "I ignore what I gotta ignore."

Unlike Joe, even in the peaceful atmosphere of the first act, Kate seems overly anxious, suspicious of Ann, obsessive about Larry, believing "signs" such as the tree blowing down: "There are meanings in such things. She goes to sleep in his room and his memorial breaks in pieces." So complacent is Joe about the past that he plays a game with the neighborhood children in which he, a "detective," will send them to a "jail" in his basement if they misbehave. Distressed by the game, Kate warns Joe that he must stop "that whole jail business!" Joe's response, "What have I got to hide?" is the first clue that there may well be something to hide. Joe and Kate, observes Stephen Centola, are "uncomfortable together" because of their shared guilt and shame.[14] A close consideration of Kate and Joe in act 1 suggests that her anxiety and his overconfidence may well forebode an eruption.

As the second act approaches a climax, George arrives, having just spoken with his father for the first time since the incarceration. George's suspicion that Joe's flu was an alibi is confirmed by Kate's slip of the tongue. Kate claims she was "misunderstood," but she and Joe come to blows. He "cruelly" accuses her of "talking like a maniac," at which "she smashes him across the face." At the end of her endurance, "beyond control," she must divulge to Chris the reason she insists that Larry is still alive: "Your brother's alive, darling, because if he's dead, your father killed him." She believes that "God does not let a son be killed by his father."

Horrified, Chris charges his father with killing the twenty-one men who flew the defective planes. Joe blames the army for improper inspection and insists he took the chance for Chris. Chris responds "with burning fury": "For me!—I was dying every day and you were killing my boys and you did it for me? What the hell do you think I was thinking of, the goddam business? Is that as far as your mind can see, the business? What is that, the world—the business? What the hell do you mean, you did it for me? Don't you have a country? Don't you live in the world?" Chris pounds his father's shoulder and, weeping, "stumbles away." He is still away at 2 A.M. the next morning, as Joe, Kate, and Ann await him. When Ann again asks Kate to accept the fact that Larry is dead, she refuses. Ann, explaining that it is her only recourse, shows Kate a letter Larry wrote her the day he died. Chris returns, bitterly admitting, "I suspected my father and I did nothing about it."

"A culture built on the market system . . . cannot escape the values [it] inculcates," notes Thomas E. Porter.[15] It is characteristic that in act 3 Joe defend his actions in terms of the market-place: "Who worked for nothin' in that war? When they work for nothin,' I'll work for nothin'. Did they ship a gun or a truck outa Detroit before they got their price? Is that clean? It's dollars and cents, nickels and dimes; war and peace, it's nickels and dimes, what's clean? Half the goddam country is gotta go if I go!" Chris's reply epitomizes past, present, and future in their relationship: "*I* know you're no worse than most men but I thought you were better. I never saw you as a man. I saw you as my father."

It is to save Chris, who is "almost breaking," that Ann gives him Larry's letter. Chris reads it aloud. Larry had learned the news about the faulty parts: "How could he have done that? Every day three or four men never come back and he sits back there doing business." Larry says that he "can't bear to live any more," is going out on a mission, and will probably be reported missing: "You mustn't wait for me," he writes; "If I had him here now I could kill him—."

As Joe prepares for the trip to jail, Kate protests that "Larry was your son too. . . . You know he'd never tell you to do this." Keller replies, looking at the letter he holds: "Then what is this if it isn't telling me? Sure, he was my son. But I think to him they were all my sons. And I guess they were, I guess they were." Joe goes into the house.

Kate insists to Chris, "The war is over!" Chris replies: "It's not enough for him to be sorry. Larry didn't kill himself to make you and Dad sorry." When Kate asks, "What more can we be!" Chris tells her: "You can be better! Once and for all you can know there's a universe of people outside and you're responsible to it, and unless you know that, you threw away your son because that's why he died." A shot is heard in the house. Only by taking his own life, as he took theirs, can Joe redeem himself to all his sons.

Barry Gross believes "Joe's suicide is less a moral judgment than an act of love," that "Joe kills himself so Chris need not kill himself. . . . Joe commits his second anti-social crime in the name of the same love that motivated the first."[16] Or it may be said that Joe's first antisocial crime was committed for Chris and his second for Larry, whose letter ends, "I could kill him."

Although Ann has been slighted by commentators who see her only as pivotal to the plot, she is a considerable person. Miller describes her as "gentle, but despite herself capable of holding fast to what she knows." She senses and then knows that Kate objects to the marriage because she believes Larry is still alive. Ann holds her ground with Kate, who insists Ann has "always been waiting" for Larry, who was not killed, only "nearly killed." Daniel Schneider sees Ann as "the messenger of death," for she produces Larry's letter about his death, which leads to Joe's.[17] But she does so only when all else fails.

Ann is now twenty-six, nearly past what was considered a marriageable age for women in those days. She tells Chris she "almost married" but changed her mind when he started to write to her. She may have been in love with Chris all along, as he has been with her—her one recollection of them as young people is of Chris and her brother George doing algebra and "Larry trying to copy my home-work." That remark and Joe's about Larry's insularity ("the world had a forty-foot front, it ended at the building line") suggest that Chris may well be a better mate. While Joe enthusiastically accepts the marriage, which he envisions in terms of a huge wedding with "tuxedoes and champagne," Kate is adamantly opposed to it as an admission of Larry's death, which might implicate Joe. Kate even packs Ann's bags when her brother George is leaving. Ann sees the marriage as her final chance for happiness. She tells Kate she has been "so lonely": "I can't leave here alone again." Larry's letter is Ann's last opportunity for a life with Chris.

The supporting roles are all significant, for Miller is an economical playwright. As in Ibsen's plays, no character appears and no line of dialogue is spoken which does not advance the action, reveal character, demonstrate theme, or achieve all three. Neighbors Lydia and Frank Lubey, who is "one year ahead of the draft," represent those who during the war could comfortably stay at home, marry, have children, and prosper, in contrast to Chris, Larry, George, and Ann. The most fully drawn minor character is Dr. Jim Bayliss, who lives next door. As his friend, Chris has encouraged Jim in the research he prefers to general practicing. But wife Sue's needs preclude his dream. Jim Bayliss "lost his best self because of a compromise with material values," notes Michael Spindler.[18]

Jim in act 3 understands Chris's dilemma, as he explains to the worried parents where Chris has gone: "Every man does have a star. The star of one's honesty. And you spend your life groping for it, but once it's out it never lights again." He feels that Chris "probably just wanted to be alone to watch his star go out." Jim reveals that he once left to do research but returned at Sue's urging: "And now I live in the usual darkness; I can't find myself."

Opening on Broadway two years after the end of World War II, *All My Sons* had a tremendous impact on critics and audiences alike. Louis Kronenberger wrote in *PM* (31 January 1947): "*All My Sons* slashes at all the defective parts of our social morality: but most of all it slashes at the unsocial nature of family loyalties, of protecting or aggrandizing the tribe at the expense of society at large." He hailed Miller as standing "easily first among our new generation of playwrights." Brooks Atkinson in the *New York Times* of 30 January 1947 praised Miller's "many-sided" talent: "Writing pithy yet unselfconscious dialogue, he has created his characters vividly, plucking them out of the run of American society, but presenting them as individuals with hearts and minds of their own. . . . He drives the play along by natural crescendo to a startling and terrifying climax."

The artistry of Miller's dialogue was generally unrecognized by the reviewers. Dennis Welland points out the frequency of questions and their effect: "The dramatic power resides in the sort of questions asked and in the inability of the characters to answer them. . . . The questions are in effect dialogue-stoppers." They also reveal "the bewilderment of a naturally garrulous man who has suddenly realized the impossibility of communication on the matters of deepest consequence."[19] "What do I do? Tell me, talk to me, what do I do?" Joe asks Kate in their final scene. When Chris returns after his angry departure, Joe inquires: "Exactly what's the matter? What's the matter? You got too much money? Is that what bothers you?"

To drive home the contrast between the comfortable familiarity of the setting and the enormity of the revelation that "business as usual" cost twenty-one lives, Miller sets the small talk of everyday suburban life against the plight of Chris's men lost on the field of battle. The family conversation revolves around the material: steak (a rarity in wartime), champagne, dresses, cars, pressure cookers. As soon as he hears that Chris and Ann plan to marry, Joe speaks of building them a stone house with a big driveway. The play's imagery, drawn from nature, also employs contrast. Kate's reliance on astrology contrasts with Jim's reference to "the star of one's honesty." The slender apple tree symbolic of Larry has been blown down the night before by a gale, which heralds the stormy action about to erupt.

At the climax of act 2, when Joe's and Kate's guilty secret is revealed, each line of dialogue between father and son mounts in intensity to Chris's final outburst. The short lines strike like machine guns firing:

CHRIS: Dad . . . Dad, you killed twenty-one men!
KELLER: What, killed?
CHRIS: You killed them, you murdered them.
KELLER: . . . How could I kill anybody?
CHRIS: Dad! Dad!
KELLER: . . . I didn't kill anybody!
CHRIS: Then explain it to me. What did you do? Explain
it to me or I'll tear you to pieces!

In contrast to the staccato of this exchange are the longer speeches—Joe's defense and Chris's accusation—with style and content differentiating each speaker. The stage directions reinforce the contrast: "Their movements now are those of subtle pursuit and escape. Keller keeps a step out of Chris's range as he talks." Joe's speech progresses by incremental repetition, the rhythm reflecting his thought processes, as if he is thinking of what to say next: "I'm in business, a man is in business; a hundred and twenty cracked, you're out of business."

Chris ends the act with the play's most significant speech. It begins with eight questions, the rising inflection in each like a sharp blow as they build to "Don't you have a country? Don't you live in the world?" He strikes Joe and then "stumbles away, covering his face as he weeps." Chris's essential humanity is revealed when he ends this powerful indictment by confessing that he doesn't know what action to take: "What must I do, Jesus God, what must I do?" A son may judge a father guilty, but how does he punish him?

The initial impact of *All My Sons* was due to its topicality, with some critics viewing it as "an exposé of war profiteering."

Harold Clurman, however, notes that this aspect of the play "represents the play's material, not its meaning. What Arthur Miller is dramatizing is a universal not a local situation. . . . The difference between Arthur Miller's individualist and the believer in 'rugged individualism' today is that the latter narrows his sense of self so that it extends no further than the family circle, while the former gives himself the scope of humanity."[20]

Notes

1. Arthur Miller, "Introduction to the *Collected Plays,*" in *The Theater Essays of Arthur Miller,* ed. Robert A. Martin (New York: Viking Press, 1978), 130–31.

2. Ibid., 129.

3. Ibid., 129–30.

4. Ibid., 132.

5. Arthur Miller, *Timebends* (New York: Grove Press, 1987), 134–35.

6. The same sentiment is expressed by Watson, a young returned soldier interviewed by Miller as a wartime reporter: "The real heroes never came back. . . . Nobody's a hero if he can still breathe." Those who return, notes Miller, "in some degree will have shared Watson's feeling of love and identity with their particular comrades and units" (Arthur Miller, *Situation Normal* [New York: Reynal and Hitchcock, 1944], 149, 156).

7. Ibid., 157.

8. Daniel E. Schneider, "A Modern Playwright: A Study of Two Plays by Arthur Miller," *The Psychoanalyst and the Artist*

ALL MY SONS

(New York: International Universities Press, 1950), 242–43. Miller recalls that in his youthful "secret vision" of family relationships, as in a chess game, the end was always "a confrontation with the father," who "could move in all directions" and whose "decree of punishment . . . was always death" (*Timebends,* 145).

9. Miller, "Introduction to the *Collected Plays,*" *Theater Essays,* 132–33.

10. Christopher Bigsby, *A Critical Introduction to Twentieth-Century American Drama: Tennessee Williams, Arthur Miller, Edward Albee* (Cambridge: Cambridge University Press, 1984), 2:167.

11. Benjamin Nelson, *Arthur Miller* (London: Peter Owen, 1970), 93.

12. Miller, *Timebends,* 134–35.

13. Miller, "Introduction to the *Collected Plays,*" *Theater Essays,* 130–31.

14. Stephen R. Centola, "Bad Faith and *All My Sons,*" in *Arthur Miller's "All My Sons": Modern Critical Interpretations,* ed. Harold Bloom (New York: Chelsea House, 1988), 130.

15. Thomas E. Porter, "The Mills of the Gods: Economics and Law in the Plays of Arthur Miller," in *Arthur Miller: New Perspectives,* ed. Robert A. Martin (Englewood Cliffs, N.J.: Prentice-Hall, 1982), 96.

16. Barry Gross, "*All My Sons* and the Larger Context," in *Critical Essays on Arthur Miller,* ed. James J. Martine (Boston: G. K. Hall, 1979), 12.

17. Schneider, "A Modern Playwright," 244.

UNDERSTANDING ARTHUR MILLER

18. Michael Spindler, "Consumer Man in Crisis: Arthur Miller's *Death of a Salesman*," *American Literature and Social Change* (London: Macmillan, 1983), 203.

19. Dennis Welland, "Two Early Plays," in *Arthur Miller's "All My Sons*," ed. Bloom, 98.

20. Harold Clurman, "The American Playwrights," *Lies like Truth* (New York: Macmillan, 1958), 66–67.

CHAPTER THREE

Death of a Salesman

Arthur Miller could hardly have anticipated the effect *Death of a Salesman* would have upon its opening-night audience in 1949. Men and women wept openly; during the intermission strangers asked in wonder how he knew their stories, or that of their father, or uncle, or brother. And this phenomenon has been repeated all over the country and all over the world. "They were weeping," Miller said in an interview with Harry Rafsky on the Canadian Broadcasting Company network in 1979, "because the central matrix of this play is . . . what most people are up against in their lives. . . . They were seeing themselves, not because Willy is a salesman, but the situation in which he stood and to which he was reacting, and which was reacting against him, was probably *the* central situation of contemporary civilization. It is that we are struggling with forces that are far greater than we can handle, with no equipment to make anything mean anything."

Miller describes the play as "Certain Private Conversations in Two Acts and a Requiem." Willy's "conversations" are interior ones, "inside his head" (once considered as a title for the play). Thus, both the past and the present are woven into one and may take place concurrently: "at that terrible moment when the voice of the past is no longer distant but quite as loud as the voice of the present. . . . The past and the present are . . . openly and vocally intertwined in his mind."[1]

In the last twenty-four hours of salesman Willy Loman's life his older son, Biff, returns home after a long absence only to reopen the conflict with his father: Biff's boyhood love for his father vanished when he discovered Willy's extramarital affair. Biff, a star athlete in high school, has become, in Willy's eyes, "a lazy bum." Willy blames his son for failing to fulfill his early promise yet suffers guilt that the shock of the affair destroyed Biff. Biff blames his father for betraying a son's trust, for excusing boyhood thefts, which have recurred as adult kleptomania, and for instilling in him the credo of wealth as success, making impossible the enjoyment of simple outdoor jobs. Wife and mother Linda tries to keep the peace between them, though her loyalty is to Willy. Younger brother Happy has taken the approved business route, starting at the bottom yet rising only to an assistant to the assistant to the manager.

As Miller points out, *Death of a Salesman* extends beyond the family circle "into society," where it "broaches . . . questions of social status, social honor and recognition." He notes that Willy has broken "the law which says that a failure in society and in business has no right to live. . . . to fail is no longer to belong to society."[2]

As Willy tries to justify his life and struggles to define where things went wrong, how ordinary past actions could have had such unforeseen and drastic present results, the changes from present to past and back again are signaled by stage lighting. When Willy is reliving the past the stage is bathed in light, with a pattern of green leaves covering the little frame house. Bygone family activities are characteristic and familiar: polishing the car, sleigh riding, playing ball, repairing the house. "How do we get back to all the great times?" Willy asks his illusory brother Ben as the play nears its end. He recalls that in the past there was a

DEATH OF A SALESMAN

future: "Always some kind of good news coming up, always something nice coming up ahead."

When present events are depicted, backlighting surrounds the house with tall, confining apartment buildings and a sky gray, darkening, or an "angry . . . orange." The action, like Willy's mind, meanders "through a world . . . well recognized by the audience," says Miller, who believes the audience, "essentially the same as myself," could identify with the "pre-existing images, events, confrontations, moods, and pieces of knowledge" that he is bringing together.[3]

As the "voice of the past" speaks as loudly to Willy as does that of the present, so the structure of the play, indicates Miller, was "determined by what was needed to draw up his [Willy's] memories like a mass of tangled roots."[4] The action opens in the present, as salesman Willy enters, "exhausted," carrying his two heavy sample cases into the small, "fragile-seeming" house closed in by apartment buildings. He has returned home at night, after having left that morning for his usual road trip from Brooklyn to New England; unable to control the car, he has been driving off the road. He is testy with his wife, Linda, who begs him to be kind to Biff, just returned home from the West. As Willy talks to himself in the kitchen, his "private conversations" begin: he is in the past, speaking to his sons as teenagers; the threatening apartment houses fade out; "the entire house and surroundings become covered with leaves."

Now Willy is reliving the happy days when Biff was the idol of the neighborhood. Lively and laughing, carrying a "borrowed" football, young Biff enters with Happpy. Willy, "laughing with him at the theft," says the coach will probably congratulate Biff for his "initiative" and thanks God that the boys are "built like Adonises. Because the man who makes an appearance in the business world, the man who creates personal interest, is the man who gets ahead. Be liked and you will never want."

There are some shadows, even in the sunny past. Although Willy brags to his sons about how "well liked" he is, he bluffs about how successful he is. When he confesses to Linda that he actually has earned a much lower commission than he boasted of, he blames it on his shortcomings. He is convinced that the seller, not the product, is important. If only he were an "Adonis," creating "personal interest," he believes he might be more successful. Willy fears that he talks too much and jokes too much, that people are laughing at his appearance. When Linda protests that he is handsome, the echoes of laughter from the Woman in the Boston hotel room are heard for the first time. As past and present intertwine, remembered events blend into present ones; a word or a sound evokes in Willy's mind an association from the past. Now the Woman appears, joking with Willy and thanking him for stockings; she fades as her laughter merges with Linda's, but she will reappear from time to time until the full incident of Biff's discovery is played out in act 2.

As the second act opens, the traveling salesman's last journey through past and present begins happily and hopefully at breakfast. Biff will call on former employer Bill Oliver, head of a sporting equipment concern, to ask for a substantial loan to start his own line of goods. Willy will ask for a desk job in New York with his firm, now run by the son of the founder. The results might have been foretold: when told that promises had been made by his father to Willy, now a veteran of thirty-four years with the company, Howard replies that there is no place for him—"business is business"—and fires him.

Willy's sons have arranged to take him to dinner at a restaurant. Biff arrives and informs Happy that, after waiting six hours, he saw Bill Oliver for one minute; he didn't remember Biff, who had been only a shipping clerk, not a salesman, as the family had always fantasized: "We've been talking in a dream for fifteen years." Worst of all, Biff, who had left Oliver's firm after stealing a carton of basketballs, now has stolen a gold fountain pen from his desk.

Biff is determined that Willy hear the truth about this encounter, but when he tells them he has been fired, Biff feeds his father's illusions by a revised version of the meeting: "I'm telling you something good." Oliver, he reports, "said it was just a question of the amount!" When Biff refuses to pursue the matter because of the fountain pen, Willy accuses him of "spiting" his father, of refusing to make good ever, in retaliation for the hotel discovery. With echoes from that past incident sounding in his ears, Willy in confusion makes his way to the washroom. Biff, "ready to weep," rushes out. Happy follows, promising two young women he has befriended in the restaurant, "we're going to paint this town!"

In the bathroom, associated in his mind with the Boston hotel, Willy is now reliving the past, when Young Biff arrived there unexpectedly to ask his father to intervene with the math teacher. Discovering the Woman, who Willy claims is only using the bathroom, Biff accuses his father: "You fake! You phony little fake!" and leaves, weeping.

The final showdown between Willy and Biff takes place near

the end of act 2. In the darkness of night Willy is planting seeds in the barren garden and is speaking to the ghost of his successful brother Ben about suicide, which would leave Biff the twenty-thousand-dollar insurance money. Ben points out, "It's called a cowardly thing, William."

WILLY: Why? Does it take more guts to stand here the rest of my life ringing up a zero?
BEN: . . . That's a point, William. . . .

And twenty thousand—that *is* something one can feel with the hand, it is there.

Biff tries to say goodbye, but Willy accuses him of cutting down his life for spite adding "and don't you dare blame it on me!" Declaring that "We never told the truth for ten minutes in this house!" Biff determines that Willy abandon the myth and face the truth: "You were never anything but a hard-working drummer who landed in the ash can like all the rest of them!" He insists, "I'm nothing, Pop. Can't you understand that? There's no spite in it any more. I'm just what I am, that's all." Biff "breaks down, sobbing, holding on to Willy." Willy, realizing that Biff loves him, "*now cries out his promise:* That boy—that boy is going to be magnificent!" Commenting on this scene, Miller notes that Biff represents Willy's "need to leave a thumbprint somewhere on the world,"[5] his "drive for a touch of immortality." His epiphany—realizing that Biff loves him—is "not only a surprising discovery but on top of it the resurrected knowledge of his union with Biff, his seed and hope. It gives him the value he needs in order to sacrifice himself."[6]

The family go up to bed, while Willy remains below for his final "private conversation" with Ben: "Loves me. [*Wonderingly:*] Always loved me. Isn't that a remarkable thing? Ben, he'll worship me for it! . . . Can you imagine that magnificence with twenty thousand dollars in his pocket?" The car is heard "starting and moving away at full speed." A short scene, "Requiem," follows. Biff, Happy, Charley, and his son Bernard are at Willy's grave with Linda, who wonders: "Why didn't anybody come?"

Willy Loman is a modern Everyman, a working man whose family and whose job come first; he will give his all for them and in return seeks love and respect. Even though he works "ten, twelve hours a day," his commissions barely keep up with the family expenses, despite his intense belief in the slogans of success he asserts to his sons: "be liked and you will never want" and "it's not what you say, it's how you say it—because personality always wins the day." Willy, observes Thomas E. Porter, is "a personification of the success myth" that prevailed in American business and society as expressed by Benjamin Franklin, Horatio Alger, and Roger Babson, who equate the "pursuit of money with the pursuit of happiness."[7] But even in the past, as Willy voices the aphorisms to which he is devoted, he confides in Linda his fear "that I'll never sell anything again, that I won't make a living for you, or a business, a business for the boys."

One of Miller's models for Willy was his uncle Manny, a short, competitive, flamboyant salesman who saw his two sons "running neck and neck" with Miller and his brother "in some race that never stopped in his mind."[8] After Manny ended his own life, Miller visited his cousin Abby in his bachelor apartment to be greeted by him in silk pajamas, accompanied by two young women. (Abby probably influenced the characterization of Happy.) "What did your pop want?" Miller asked his cousin, who "filled with the roiling paradoxes of love for me and competitive resentment, of contempt for his late failed father and at the same time a pitying love," replied, "He wanted a business for us. So we could all work together. . . . A business for the boys."[9]

Willy regards his older brother Ben as "success incarnate," a man who "knew what he wanted and went out and got it! Walked into a jungle, and comes out, the age of twenty-one, and he's rich!" Although his own financial struggles should lead Willy to at least question the myth, he continues to pursue it, to insist that to "get ahead" in the business world all one needs is a good appearance and personality. He teaches Young Biff and Happy that athletic ability is more important than learning, praises Biff for his "ingenuity" in stealing, and laughs when he ridicules his math teacher.

As the real and the unreal merge in Willy's mind, so "an air of the dream," says Miller in describing the setting, "clings to the place, a dream rising out of reality." Willy's description in act 2 of salesman Dave Singleman is a dream of "those days," hardly applicable to present reality. Willy would never have insisted on a desk job had he recognized that in the real business world there is no place for the old who can no longer pull their weight. In the past it was Singleman's example that led Willy to become a salesman and abandon the idea of seeking gold in Alaska, of pursuing the frontier to find riches (another American dream): "I realized that selling was the greatest career a man could want. 'Cause what could be more satisfying than to be able to go, at the age of eighty-four, into twenty or thirty different cities, and pick

DEATH OF A SALESMAN

up a phone, and be remembered and loved and helped by so many different people?" Willy relates that when Dave died "the death of a salesman," on the train to Boston, his funeral was attended by "hundreds of salesmen and buyers."

If Willy could separate the real world from his business dreamworld (which hardly accords with Ben's advice to Biff: "Never fight fair with a stranger, boy. You'll never get out of the jungle that way"), he might better adjust to both worlds. But when the myths on which he has staked so much fail to come true, "he attempts to paper over reality with the myth. He allows the dreams necessary to his work to start to take over his whole person," observes Jeremy Hawthorn. "Willy . . . has never realized that his dreams are dreams, and may offer him some comfort for the life he has to lead, but can never actually be lived."[10] In explaining the character of Willy to members of the Chinese cast, Miller pointed out: "He cannot bear reality, and since he can't do much to change it, he keeps changing his ideas of it. . . . You must look beyond his ludicrousness to what he is actually confronting. . . . There is a nobility, in fact, in Willy's struggle. Maybe it comes from his refusal ever to relent, to give up."[11]

Willy's many contradictions reflect his inability to distinguish between the dream of success and the reality of the world around him. In the opening scene Willy first describes Biff as "a lazy bum," but when Linda suggests that "he's still lost," Willy insists: "In the greatest country in the world a young man with such—personal attractiveness, gets lost. And such a hard worker. There's one thing about Biff—he's not lazy." Although he is always optimistic with the boys, Willy confides to Ben in act 1 that "Dad left when I was such a baby and I never had a chance to talk to him and I still feel—kind of temporary about myself." Insecurity lurks beneath his confidence in personality and appearance as the keys to success. He seeks Ben's advice about the boys: "I'm afraid that I'm not teaching them the right kind of— Ben, how should I teach them?" Gerald Weales observes that "Willy Loman is a character so complex, so contradictory, so vulnerable, so insensitive, so trusting, so distrustful, so blind, so aware—in short, so human—that he forces man on us by being one."[12]

Death of a Salesman has been described as "a tragedy of the common man," in which the hero's error in judgment lies in his unquestioning commitment to a career of selling himself. In Miller's opinion a true tragic figure must be committed: the hero's "commitment to his course" is one of "intensity, the human passion to surpass his given bounds, the fanatic insistence upon his self-conceived role."[13] Yet Miller questions whether *Death of a Salesman* may not have become "simply too threatening" for today's audiences: "I wonder whether there isn't a certain . . . softness, or else a genuine inability to face the tough decisions and the dreadful results of error. . . . You need a certain amount of confidence to watch tragedy. If you yourself are about to die, you're not going to see that play."[14]

Miller has always regarded his salesman as "heroic," he says, replying to charges that Willy lacks the "stature" of a tragic hero. He points out that a modern hero need not be high-born as in classical days, when most people were "divested of alternatives"; today it is a question of stature, not of rank. "So long as the hero may be said to have had alternatives of a magnitude to have materially changed the course of his life, it seems to me that . . . he cannot be debarred from the heroic role." Another aspect of Miller's definition of modern tragedy is "a revelation of . . . the operations of an ethic, of social laws of action no less powerful in their effects upon individuals than any tribal law administered by gods with names."[15] Not only is Willy "shaped by a society that believed . . . in the myth of success," Thomas E. Porter points out, but "he has become the agent and the representative of that society."[16]

In discussing Willy's death, Miller points out that "even death, the ultimate negative," can be "an assertion of bravery." He notes that "Willy Loman is filled with a joy, however broken-hearted," for "he has achieved a very powerful piece of knowledge, which is that he is loved by his son and has been embraced by him and forgiven. In this he is given his existence, so to speak—his fatherhood, for which he has always striven and which until now he could not achieve." That the victory "closes the circle for him and propels him to his death, is the wage of his sin, which was to have committed himself so completely to the counterfeits of dignity and the false coinage embodied in his idea of success that he can prove his existence only by bestowing 'power' on his posterity, a power deriving from the sale of his last asset, himself, for the price of his insurance policy."[17]

Harold Bloom sees Willy as "slain by his need for love, for familial love. . . . Love kills Loman—Linda's love . . . contains very little understanding of him, and Biff's love is so masked by ambivalence that Willy is doomed to interpret it wrongly." "Excessive love," theirs without understanding and his own, has sent Willy "into the desert of himself, there to wander as an exile from the only affections that could sustain and save him." Miller, observes Bloom, "has an immense capacity for the dramatic representation of the destructive sorrows of familial love."[18]

If Willy dies clinging to his dream and Happpy pledges to carry it out for him, at least Biff is able at last to shake it off. Heretofore, his enjoyment of the outdoor simple life has been marred whenever he recalls his father's expectations of him. In the first scene he lyrically describes his work to Happy: "There's nothing more inspiring or—beautiful than the sight of a mare and a new colt." But then his guilt at betraying the American dream takes over: "What the hell am I doing playing around with horses, twenty-eight dollars a week! I'm thirty-four years old, I oughta be makin' my future. That's when I come running home." He urges Happy to join him out West, "if you were with me I'd be happy out there. . . . The trouble is we weren't brought up to grub for money." (They were brought up to believe that money was bestowed upon an "Adonis" who was "well liked.")

Biff realizes that the business world and the success myth are not for him: "We don't belong in this nuthouse of a city! We should be mixing cement on some open plain, or—or carpenters." Willy, he notes sadly in the Requiem scene, had practically reconstructed the little house with his own hands— the stoop, the porch, the garage. "There's more of him in that front stoop than in all the sales he ever made."

Miller explains the character of Biff to the Chinese actor playing the role in Beijing: "Away from home he sometimes feels a painfully unrequited love for his father, a sense of something unfinished between them bringing feelings of guilt." Miller tells him, "Biff knows very well what he wants, but Willy and his idea

DEATH OF A SALESMAN

of success disapprove of what he wants, and this is the basic reason you [Biff] have returned here—to somehow resolve this conflict with your father, to get his blessing, to be able to cast off his heavy hand and free yourself."[19]

In his final showdown with Willy, Biff asserts, "you blew me so full of hot air I could never stand taking orders from anybody! . . . I had to be boss big shot in two weeks, and I'm through with it!" As he ran down the office building's eleven flights with the stolen fountain pen, says Biff, he stopped: "And I saw—the sky. I saw the things that I love in this world." He asked himself, "Why am I trying to become what I don't want to be? . . . when all I want is out there, waiting for me the minute I say I know who I am!"

Except for Linda, the other principals in the cast are fathers, sons, and brothers, contrasts to Willy and Biff—Charley, Willy's good neighbor and friend, his son Bernard, sons Happy Loman and Howard Wagner, and brother Ben, who has seven sons. Miller explained to the Chinese cast of *Salesman* that "the one red line connecting everyone in the play was a love for Willy; not admiration, necessarily, but a kind of visceral recognition that in his fumbling and often ridiculous way he is trying to lift up a belief in immense redeeming human possibilities. . . . He is forever signaling to a future that he cannot describe and will not live to see, but he is in love with it all the same."[20]

Charley is Willy's only friend, as Willy admits in Charley's office in act 2. Yet the two are always bickering, because, Charley tells Willy, when he rejects his friend's job offer, "You been jealous of me all your life, you damned fool!" A successful businessman, Charley is the opposite of Willy, who insists that it is important to be "impressive and well liked." "Who liked J. P.

Morgan?" Charley retorts. "In a Turkish bath he'd look like a butcher. But with his pockets on he was very well liked." Charley attempts unsuccessfully to make Willy differentiate between reality and fantasy. When Willy is bewildered that young Howard not only lacked gratitude but actually fired him, Charley comments: "Willy, when're you gonna realize that them things don't mean anything? You named him Howard, but you can't sell that. The only thing you got in this world is what you can sell. And the funny thing is that you're a salesman, and you don't know that."

Willy learns that Charley's son Bernard, now a lawyer, is arguing a case before the Supreme Court; he is impressed: "The Supreme Court! And he didn't even mention it!" Charley replies, "He don't have to—he's gonna do it." As Willy wonders: "And you never told him what to do, did you? You never took any interest in him," Charley responds, "My salvation is that I never took any interest in anything."

If Charley, who is giving Willy fifty dollars a week as a "loan," represents a successful businessman who is caring, young Howard Wagner is just the opposite. As he rejects and finally fires Willy, Howard speaks in the jargon and platitudes of the marketplace: "You're a road man, Willy, and we do a road business." "If I had a spot, I'd slam you right in." "It's a business, kid, and everybody's gotta pull his own weight."

Younger son and brother Happy has entered the business world but after a number of years is still only an assistant to an assistant. His nickname has become ironic. He tells Biff in their bedroom in act 1: "Sometimes I want to just rip my clothes off in the middle of the store and outbox that goddam merchandise manager. I mean I can outbox, outrun, and outlift anybody in that store, and I have to take orders from those common, petty sons-

meekly behind her husband, wiping up after him. She has strength; she has held this family together and she knows this very well. . . . It is she who is marshaling the forces, such as they are, that might save Willy."[22]

In contrast to Linda is the Woman (Miss Francis) in the hotel room. Throughout the play, as Willy recalls the past, the encounter haunts him in snatches, until the scene is played out in the restaurant sequence in act 2. Willy has confessed his loneliness on the road to her, to Linda, and finally to Biff. Miss Francis is a receptionist (Willy promotes her to a buyer in his explanation) who also is lonely. Single and about Willy's age, she chose Willy for his sense of humor and promises to put him through to the buyers. Willy's guilt is compounded by his gifts to her of stockings, "two boxes of size nine sheers." Because women's nylon stockings were a luxury during and after World War II, the fact that Linda is always mending her stockings infuriates Willy and deepens his guilt.

All of the women, including the two in the restaurant and Charley's secretary, are contrasted to Linda, whose character Miller defines when she first appears: "Most often jovial, she has developed an iron repression of her exceptions to Willy's behavior—she more than loves him, she admires him, as though his mercurial nature, his temper, his massive dreams and little cruelties, served her only as sharp reminders of the turbulent longings within him, longings which she shares but lacks the temperament to utter and follow to their end."

Yet she cannot understand, she says at Willy's grave, why he has killed himself. Her role in the marriage is that of a "homemaker" (a 1940s term) who loves and admires her husband. As

of-bitches till I can't stand it any more." Happy has bought his father's dream. His Dave Singleman is the merchandise manager: "When he walks into the store the waves part in front of him. That's fifty-two thousand dollars a year coming through the revolving door, and I got more in my pinky finger than he's got in his head." Happy's dream is "to walk into the store the way he walks in."

Like Willy, Happy condones dishonesty: he takes bribes from sellers to favor them with an order and seduces the fiancées of his bosses as one-upmanship. Although his management skills are not apparent, his ability to charm women is displayed in the restaurant scene. To score a point in sibling rivalry, he convinces a model to break a date and to get a friend for Biff. Happy, like Willy and perhaps Miller, is the unfavored younger son who compensates by seeking love outside the family that has lavished praise and attention on the elder brother. In the Requiem scene it is apparent that Willy's dream lives on. When Biff claims, "He had the wrong dreams," Happy asserts: "I'm gonna show you and everybody else that Willy Loman did not die in vain. He had a good dream. It's the only dream you can have—to come out number-one man. He fought it out here, and this is where I'm gonna win it for him."

While the men leave home for work and for sporting and social events, Linda is never seen away from the house. In Willy's reliving of earlier days, Linda mends clothing, carries wash, and keeps the household accounts. In action of the present she is the supporter and defender of Willy in the clashes with her sons. In the opening scene, as they complain of Willy's behavior, she asserts: "he's the dearest man in the world to me, and I won't have anyone making him feel unwanted and low and blue." Linda, who loves Willy, states the case for him and those like him who work for the sake of their families: "I don't say he's a great man. Willy Loman never made a lot of money. His name was never in the paper. He's not the finest character that ever lived. But he's a human being, and a terrible thing is happening to him. So attention must be paid. He's not to be allowed to fall into his grave like an old dog. Attention, attention must be finally paid to such a person." When Biff and Happy return after deserting Willy in the restaurant, she throws their flowers on the floor and chastises them: "Pick up this stuff, I'm not your maid any more. Pick it up, you bum, you!" Willy's inconsiderate treatment of her angers Biff, who has witnessed Willy's infidelity.

Although Linda has always seen through Willy's bragging and his false dreams, she loves him enough to realize that she would never be able to change him. She encourages him in his exaggerated views of himself as father and breadwinner, for she recognizes the insecurity that prompts them. After Willy has boasted to Young Biff and Happy of his successful trip and brags of selling in the thousands, Linda asks, "Did you sell anything?" Willy at first reports a gross of twelve hundred, but as Linda begins to figure their bills, he confesses to two hundred gross, then complains:

WILLY: My God, if business don't pick up I don't know what I'm gonna do!

LINDA: Well, next week you'll do better.

WILLY: Oh, I'll knock 'em dead next week. I'll go to Hartford. I'm very well liked in Hartford.

In act 2 Linda discourages Willy from acceptin￼ to manage his timberland in Alaska. No doubt she is￼ Willy might desert his family for fortune hunting, like￼ and brother before him. She assures Willy, "You're d￼ enough." When Ben asks her, "Enough for what, m￼ Linda replies: "Enough to be happy right here, right n￼ WILLY, *while* BEN *laughs:*] Why must everybody conqu￼ world? You're well liked, and the boys love you, and someo￼ [*to* BEN]—why, old man Wagner told him just the other day￼ if he keeps it up he'll be a member of the firm, didn't he, Will￼ When Willy tells Ben, "I am building something with this firm￼ Ben asks, "What are you building? Lay your hand on it. Wher￼ is it?"

Willy rejects Ben's job offer and repeats the success formula to which he is committed: "It's not what you do, Ben. It's who you know and the smile on your face! It's contacts, Ben, contacts! The whole wealth of Alaska passes over the lunch table at the Commodore Hotel, and that's the wonder, the wonder of this country, that a man can end with diamonds here on the basis of being liked!"

Kay Stanton points out that "the Loman men are all less than they hold themselves to be, but Linda is more than she is credited to be. . . . She is the foundation that has allowed the Loman men to build themselves up, if only in dreams, and she is the support that enables them to continue despite their failures. . . . She represents human dignity and values: cooperative, moral, human behavior as opposed to lawless assertion of self over all others through assumed superiority."[21] Miller explains the character to the actress playing Linda in Bejing: "She is not a woman to follow

Willy is most often on the road, she holds the home together, cares for the boys, cooks the food, buys, washes, and mends the clothing, and, most of all, worries about money, whether there will be enough to cover the mortgage and the insurance and the innumerable repairs. Even in his best days Willy's commissions barely paid their expenses; emergencies are near disasters: "To fix the hot water," she tells Happy, who contributes only fifty dollars at Christmas, "it cost ninety-seven fifty!" Much of her conversation with Willy revolves around household repairs; when there are celebrations, such as Biff's big day at Ebbets Field, she is left behind. She wonders in the Requiem why Willy would take his life when their biggest monthly worry, the mortgage, finally has been paid off that very day. "We're free and clear" are words she has never yet uttered in all the years of their marriage. Now it is too late: "And there'll be nobody home."

The play's symbolism is built on contrasts: the everyday and familiar with the faraway and unattainable, the happy camaraderie of the past with the lonely, frustrating present, dreams with reality, and the destructive, self-centered law of the jungle with love. Miller states in his introduction that "the play grew from simple images. From a little frame house on a street of little frame houses, which had once been loud with the noise of growing boys, and then was empty and silent and finally occupied by strangers." Other images include the car: "Where is that car now? And the chamois cloths carefully washed and put up to dry, where are the chamois cloths?"[23]

The image of the house in the happy past, set in green leaves, is accompanied by a haunting melody on the flute. Nature and the outdoors characterize the past, when the house stood in tree-lined fields. In the present, with apartment buildings closing in, it is impossible to plant anything in the yard, although Willy tries to do so on his last day. The picture of him with a flashlight in the night, planting carrot, beet, and lettuce seeds in the infertile earth, sums up the futility of his life and of the heritage he leaves his "seed."

In contrast to the city is the frontier. Selling his handmade flutes, Willy's father traveled by wagon with his family to the West and thence by himself, when Willy was a baby, to Alaska. At three Willy was left in South Dakota by Ben, who sought his father in Alaska but ended up in Africa, where he grew rich. Asked his advice on how to teach Willy's boys, the ghostly Ben replies: "William, when I walked into the jungle, I was seventeen. When I walked out I was twenty-one. And, by God, I was rich!" Willy responds: "That's just the spirit I want to imbue them with! To walk into a jungle!"

In contrast to Willy's insubstantial dreams, Ben's diamond mines in Africa are symbolic of solid, substantial wealth, like the twenty thousand dollars in insurance that will be Willy's legacy to Biff, who Willy predicts will be "magnificent." Ben agrees: "Yes, outstanding, with twenty thousand behind him." He reminds Willy that "The jungle is dark but full of diamonds," and that "a diamond is rough and hard to the touch." Here the jungle (and its darkness) may symbolize death, but throughout the play, in association with Ben, it represents the industrial marketplace. Although he tells Happy, "Screw the business world!" Biff steals emblems of the executive: a suit and a gold fountain pen.

While the frontiers, timberlands, diamonds, and the jungle symbolize the unattainable and the exotic, the car, the hot water heater, and the refrigerator, which are always breaking down, represent everyday life and its struggles and frustrations. "Who ever heard of a Hastings refrigerator?" asks Willy, whose purchase was prompted by the "biggest ads." Unaware of the analogy to himself, he complains, "When you finally paid for them, they're used up." The image of life-giving water in the tank is contrasted to the symbol of suicide which Linda discovers, the black rubber pipe with an attachment that fits the gas pipe on the heater.

The kitchen is another of the "simple images" from which the play grew, says Miller, "and the endless, convoluted discussions, wonderments, arguments, belittlements, encouragements, fiery resolutions, abdications . . . and all in the kitchen now occupied by strangers who cannot hear what the walls are saying."[24] The house furniture on stage consists only of pieces used in the action: the chairs, table, and refrigerator in the kitchen and the beds in the bedrooms. The single decorative item is Biff's "silver athletic trophy" on a shelf over the bed. The sparseness of the furnishings is indicative of Miller's economy as a playwright—not one property is present which does not contribute a meaning beyond the literal; the same is true of his dialogue and action. Probably the most evocative of the symbols is the car. Family pride and community are epitomized in the weekend polishing and outings. But the car is also the instrument by which traveling salesman Willy earns his living, and, like him, it wears out. Finally, it is the means of his self-afflicted death and of the inheritance he leaves his son.

Because *Death of a Salesman* is so true to life, it is seldom noticed that Miller's dialogue is not realistic; it is heightened, poetic realism. When Willy is remembering the happy past, his speech may be rhapsodic, like his description of New England towns to his sons in act 1. His longest speech, in the hostile setting of Howard's office, is his lyrical eulogy of salesman Dave Singleman. In contrast to its long, rhythmic sentences, Howard's monosyllabic business jargon is short and sharp, fired with machine-gun rapidity. Questions abound in Willy's dialogue and in Linda's, reinforcing their insecurity, living on the edge, struggling from payment to payment, on the car, the house, the insurance.

A reminder of the swift passage of time sounds throughout the play, like a leitmotif. Neither Howard nor Ben has time for Willy. Howard rushes Willy out: "I need the office," while Ben is always looking at his watch and cannot wait. His last words to Willy are: "Time, William. Time!" and "The boat. We'll be late." Concern with time reinforces the theme of change; everything is growing old, wearing out, as is Willy himself. One of the most poignant images is Willy's statement to Ben that he feels "kind of temporary" about himself, symbolizing the air of unreality, the atmosphere of a dream, of living as Miller has stated "on the edge of the abyss." In this insubstantial pageant Biff represents the "thumbprint" Willy wishes to leave behind him.

Miller concludes his introduction to *Death of a Salesman* by observing that "Willy's law," the belief "that a failure in society and in business has no right to live," a belief that "administers guilt to him," is a "deeply suspect 'good,'" whose value the play questions. By doing so, it "serves more to raise our anxieties than to reassure us of the existence of an unseen but humane meta-physical system in the world." Miller attempts "to counter this anxiety with an opposing system which, so to speak, is in a race for Willy's faith, and it is the system of love which is the opposite of the law of success. It is embodied in Biff Loman, but by the time Willy can perceive his love it can serve only as an ironic comment on the life he sacrificed for power and for success and its tokens."[25]

Notes

1. Arthur Miller, "Introduction to the *Collected Plays*," in *The Theater Essays of Arthur Miller*, ed. Robert A. Martin (New York: Viking Press, 1978), 138.

2. Arthur Miller, "The Family in Modern Drama," *Theater Essays*, 74; "Introduction to the *Collected Plays*," *Theater Essays*, 149.

3. Miller, "Introduction to the *Collected Plays*," *Theater Essays*, 152, 137.

4. Ibid., 138.

5. Ibid., 142.

6. Arthur Miller, *"Salesman" in Beijing* (New York: Viking Press, 1984), 170.

7. Thomas E. Porter, "Acres of Diamonds: *Death of a Salesman*," *Myth and Modern American Drama* (Detroit: Wayne State University Press, 1969), 128–29.

8. Arthur Miller, *Timebends* (New York: Grove Press, 1987), 122.

9. Ibid., 129–30.

10. Jeremy Hawthorn, "Sales and Solidarity," in *Willy Loman*, ed. Harold Bloom (New York: Chelsea House, 1991), 94–95.

11. Miller, *"Salesman" in Beijing*, 27.

12. Gerald Weales, "Arthur Miller in the 1960s," in *Arthur Miller: New Perspectives,* ed. Robert A. Martin (Englewood Cliffs, N.J.: Prentice-Hall, 1982), 98.

13. Miller, "Introduction to the *Collected Plays,*" *Theater Essays,* 146.

14. Olga Carlisle and Rose Styron, "Arthur Miller: An Interview," in *Theater Essays* ed. Martin, 270–71.

15. Miller, "Introduction to the *Collected Plays,*" *Theater Essays,* 144–46.

16. Porter, "Acres of Diamonds," 134.

17. Miller, "Introduction to the *Collected Plays,*" *Theater Essays,* 147.

18. Bloom, *Willy Loman,* 1, 3.

19. Miller, *"Salesman" in Beijing,* 79, 71.

20. Ibid., 49.

21. Kay Stanton, "Women and the American Dream of *Death of a Salesman,*" in Bloom, *Willy Loman,* 135, 137.

22. Miller, *"Salesman" in Bejing,* 69.

23. Miller, "Introduction to the *Collected Plays,*" *Theater Essays,* 141–42.

24. Ibid., 142.

25. Ibid., 149–50.

CHAPTER FOUR

The Crucible

In *The Crucible* John Proctor is an ordinary man who achieves an extraordinary moral victory when he is tested in the crucible of the 1692 Salem witch trials. In his struggle against his society's mass hysteria and their authoritarian court, he loses his life, but he preserves his integrity, his "name."

Miller has stated that the impetus for his plays has always been "what was in the air." In the early 1950s it was the hearings of the powerful House Un-American Activities Committee, which decreed that the American Communist Party (a legal political party) was endangering the nation. Party members, "fellow travellers," and indeed anyone believed to be favorable toward Russia (a U.S. ally in World War II and enemy afterward) could be summoned before the committee to confess and recant his or her former sympathies and to name friends and associates thought to favor communism, Marxism, or socialism.

Reading Marion Starkey's *The Devil in Massachusetts,* Miller, like many others, was struck by the analogy to the committee hearings: "The main point . . . precisely as in seventeenth-century Salem, was that the accused make public confession, damn his confederates as well as his Devil master, and guarantee his sterling new allegiance by breaking disgusting old vows. . . . not in solemn privacy but out in the public air. . . . It came down to a government decree of *moral* guilt that could easily be made to disappear by ritual speech: intoning names of fellow sinners and recanting former beliefs."[1]

Before journeying to Salem to consult the court records of the witch trials, Miller had his "central image" in mind: "A guilt-ridden man, John Proctor, who, having slept with his teen-age servant girl, watches with horror as she becomes the leader of the witch-hunting pack and points her accusing finger at the wife he has himself betrayed." In Salem he found "the hard evidence of what had become my play's center: the breakdown of the Proctor marriage and Abigail Williams's determination to get Elizabeth murdered so that she could have John."[2]

Searching for motives in the actual records, Miller noted "the sexual theme, either open or barely concealed. . . . Here was guilt, the guilt of illicit sexuality. . . . Had there been no tinder of guilt to set aflame, had the cult and culture of repression not ruled so tightly, no outbreak would have been possible. John Proctor, then, in being driven to confess not to a metaphoric guilt but to actual sex with an identified teenage partner, might save the community in the only way possible—by raising to consciousness what had been suppressed and in holy disguise was out to murder them all."[3]

Miller also finds a parallel in "the guilt, two centuries apart, of holding illicit, suppressed feelings of alienation and hostility toward standard, daylight society as defined by its most orthodox proponents."[4] That the people's terror could be so manipulated by an outside force such as the committee or the Salem court, observes Miller, was due to "the sense of guilt which individuals strive to conceal by complying. . . . Conscience was no longer a private matter but one of state administration. I saw men handing conscience to other men and thanking other men for the opportunity of doing so." Miller says he wished to write a play that would "show that the sin of public terror is that it divests man of conscience, of himself."[5]

In *The Crucible* the sexual repression of the times drives a group of teenage girls to secret outings in the woods, where they dance naked. When Minister Parris spies them, guilt and fright cause two of them, Ruth Putnam and Betty Parris, either to pretend or experience catatonia. The opening scene takes place the following day at the home of Parris, where his daughter Betty lies mysteriously ill. News spreads fast, hymn-singing villagers crowd the parlor below, and Reverend Hale arrives, summoned as an expert on witchcraft. As the girls are questioned, Abigail, to clear her own name, accuses, as a tool of the Devil, Parris's black West Indian servant Tituba.

When John Proctor enters, seeking his young servant Mary Warren, Miller describes him: evidence suggests that "he had a sharp and biting way with hypocrites. . . . even-tempered, and not easily led. . . . a man in his prime . . . with a quiet confidence and an unexpressed, hidden force." A brief exchange between Abigail and Proctor alone together reveals her desire for John, her hatred of his wife, Elizabeth (who discharged Abigail when the affair was discovered), and his determination not to resume the relationship.

Reverend Hale, assisted by Parris and landowner Thomas Putnam (who cunningly plants names of his enemies in Tituba's distracted mind), urges Tituba to "confess" to witchcraft and to name others she has seen with the Devil. She names the very persons Putnam suggested. "Abigail rises, staring as though inspired, and cries out." She names the same women and adds others. Betty Parris, aroused, joins in. Putnam calls for the marshal to arrest the accused, Hale instructs that irons be brought, and, as the girls' "ecstatic cries" continue, the curtain falls on the first act.

In introducing the play Miller explains that the theocracy of Salem was "a combine of state and religious power whose function was to keep the community together, and to prevent any kind of disunity that might open it to destruction by material or ideological enemies." But in time the repressions "were heavier than seemed warranted." The witch hunt "was a perverse manifestation of the panic which set in . . . when the balance began to turn toward greater individual freedom." Outspoken against authority, John Proctor criticizes Parris for materialism and Putnam for fraudulent land claims. The witch hunt, observes Miller, provided an opportunity for expressing "long-held hatreds of neighbors"; in the "general revenge" land lust was "elevated to the arena of morality."

The rapidity in act 1 with which frightened teenagers become respected accusers characterizes the speed of the full-blown investigation under way eight days later. With great economy Miller sketches a short domestic scene of tension and bitterness between Elizabeth and John which opens the second act. Their servant Mary, now "an official of the court," reports that Abigail leads the girls into the court: "And folks are brought before them, and if they scream and howl and fall to the floor— the person's clapped in the jail for bewitchin' them." Four judges have been sent from Boston, headed by the deputy governor of the province, Danforth.

Hale arrives on a mission; he is visiting those the accusers have "mentioned," among them Elizabeth and seventy-year-old

THE CRUCIBLE

Rebecca Nurse, charged because her offspring live while Ann Putnam's died in infancy. The marshal appears with a warrant for Elizabeth, named by Abigail for inflicting bodily harm on her when the girl "discovered" a needle in her stomach. When he searches the room and finds a "poppet" (doll) with a needle, Mary reveals they are hers: "Ask Abby, Abby sat beside me when I made it." Proctor rips up the arrest warrant: "Is the accuser always holy now?" He warns that "vengeance is walking Salem," that "the little crazy children are jangling the keys of the kingdom, and common vengeance writes the law!" Elizabeth is led away by the marshal; the act ends with Proctor insisting to a sobbing Mary that she must tell the the court the truth, that the girls have seen no spirits.

As act 3 begins, Proctor and Mary present to Judges Danforth and Hathorne her deposition that the girls are pretending. Claiming that Mary lies, Abigail even threatens Danforth himself, until Proctor, desperate to prove the truth, calls her a whore and confesses his sin: "I have known her." He charges that "She thinks to dance with me on my wife's grave!" When Danforth questions Elizabeth, who Proctor has claimed never lies, she denies that "John Proctor ever committed the crime of lechery."

Hale begs Danforth to stop—"Private vengeance is working through this testimony"—but Abigail and the screaming girls denounce Mary until she joins with them and accuses Proctor. Ordered to confess his "black allegiance" to the Devil, Proctor implicates not only Danforth but also himself and all who stand by inactive as hysteria grips Salem: "I hear the boot of Lucifer, I see his filthy face! And it is my face, and yours, Danforth! For them that quail to bring men out of ignorance, as I have quailed, and as you quail now when you know in all your black hearts that this be fraud—God damns our kind especially, and we will burn, we will burn together!"

Penelope Curtis points out that the dramatic impact of this scene depends on the way "the communication of hysteria from one person to another creates a dramatic illusion of a quasi-impersonal force, more powerful and more malignant than its individual agents. . . . What we see is not just 'mass' but institutionalized hysteria. . . . While the girls seem genuinely beside themselves, the outcome of their actions looks so very calculated. . . . [There is] that strange dual impression of incalculable factors in a situation mysteriously beyond control, and an outcome at once monstrous and precise: *a possessed commmunity.*"[6]

Although the emotional climax has been reached, the tension does not abate in the final act. The cell, the darkness, and the cold create an atmosphere of despair. Hale has been praying with the seven condemned to hang that morning, including Rebecca and John. As they have refused to confess and save their lives, he reports to Danforth: "You must pardon them. They will not budge." Nor will Danforth budge: "I cannot pardon these when twelve are already hanged for the same crime. It is not just." Danforth believes "Postponement now speaks a floundering on my part; reprieve or pardon must cast doubt upon the guilt of them that died till now."

Although at the time the American Bar Association protested the portrayal of Danforth,[7] Miller stated later that he had attempted in the third act to show Danforth as disposed "at least to listen to arguments that go counter to the line of the prosecution. There is no such swerving in the record, and I think now,"

THE CRUCIBLE

he says, "that I was wrong in mitigating the evil of this man. . . . Instead, I would perfect his evil to its utmost" as "a thematic consideration." "There are people dedicated to evil in the world," he continues; "without their perverse example we should not know the good. Evil is not a mistake but a fact in itself."[8]

Elizabeth, whose life is being spared in prison because she is pregnant, is led in. Hale asks her to urge John to confess because "if he is taken I count myself his murderer." In chains John is brought from the dungeon to encounter Elizabeth alone. "He is another man, bearded, filthy, his eyes misty as though webs had overgrown them." The earlier climax took place on a crowded stage, noisy with the screams of the girls; now the resolution of the pair's emotional crisis begins quietly. In contrast to their domestic scene in act 2, bitterness, blame, and distrust are gone; their love has matured beyond the physical, into humble appreciation of the other's worth and self-awareness of one's own shortcomings. John asks Elizabeth's forgiveness. She replies, "John, it come to naught that I should forgive you, if you'll not forgive yourself." She assures him, "Whatever you will do, it is a good man does it . . . I have read my heart this three month, John. [*Pause.*] I have sins of my own to count. It needs a cold wife to prompt lechery."

John resolves to confess and save his life: "I think it is honest, I think so; I am no saint. . . . Let Rebecca go like a saint; for me it is fraud!" John's deposition has been written out, and Rebecca is led in to see him declare that he bound himself to the Devil. Danforth asks John if he ever saw Rebecca Nurse or others with the Devil, and John answers no each time. When Danforth insists that many have testified that they saw Rebecca with the Devil, John replies: "They think to go like saints. I like not to spoil their names." When he is ordered to sign his testimony, he does so. Then he snatches it up: "God does not need my name nailed upon the church! God sees my name; God knows how black my sins are!" Insisting he will not be used, Proctor declares: "I have three children—how may I teach them to walk like men in the world, and I sold my friends?"

> DANFORTH: You have not sold your friends—
> PROCTOR: Beguile me not! I blacken all of them when this is nailed to the church the very day they hang for silence!

John will not relinquish the signed confession:

> Because it is my name! Because I cannot have another in my life! Because I lie and sign myself to lies! Because I am not worth the dust on the feet of them that hang! How may I live without my name? I have given you my soul; leave me my name!

When Danforth warns that John must either hand over the signed confession or hang, John tears the paper; "he is weeping in fury, but erect." Hale, fearing another murder on his head, cautions: "Man, you will hang! You cannot!" to which John replies:

> I can. And there's your first marvel, that I can. You have made your magic now, for now I do think I see some shred of goodness in John Proctor. Not enough to weave a banner with, but white enough to keep it from such dogs.

THE CRUCIBLE

Robert Hogan observes, "In the life of John Proctor, one single action is decisive, dominating, and totally pertinent, and this action, this moment of decision and commitment, is that climax towards which every incident in the play tends."[9] The drumrolls sound for the hanging; Proctor and Rebecca start out toward the gallows. Parris and Hale plead with Elizabeth to stop John. At the bars of the window she speaks the last lines: "He have his goodness now. God forbid I take it from him!"

If *Death of a Salesman* is a "tragedy of the common man," *The Crucible* presents as hero a common man with uncommon qualities. On his first entrance John is visually impressive, being "powerful of body." Only he maintains a "steady manner" in the midst of the growing hysteria, and he is forthright with the minister Parris and the landowner Putnam. The girls react to his sexual magnetism: Mercy is "strangely titillated," and, when Proctor is alone with Abigail, their earlier affair is revealed.

In introducing Proctor, Miller suggests a tragic flaw: "He is a sinner, a sinner not only against the moral fashion of the time, but against his own vision of decent conduct. . . . Proctor, respected and even feared in Salem, has come to regard himself as a kind of fraud." The community, like that in *Oedipus,* is suffering, a condition whose cause must be "proportionate," insists Hale in act 2, when Proctor charges that it is not witchcraft but Abby's "vengeance" at work: "The world goes mad, and it profit nothing you should lay the cause to the vengeance of a little girl." The "cause proportionate," Hale suggests, could be blasphemy or murder, or—unwittingly alluding to Proctor—"abomination."

Not only has Proctor sinned against his own standards of decent conduct, but he also suffers guilt for jeopardizing

Elizabeth's life, for he realizes that Abby aims to replace her after she is hanged. At the end of act 2 Proctor believes he can thwart Abby and save Elizabeth by Mary's admission that the girls have lied. But Elizabeth assumes some blame, as she admits in the final scene that her coldness prompted his lechery. Nor will she judge Proctor or help him decide whether to live by confessing to the lie of witchcraft or to lose his life but save the community by revealing that the trials are a fraud. He finds his integrity in making his choice and in preserving his "name," his identity, although he must die to do so. Unlike Willy, Proctor arrives at the self-realization that defines classical tragic heroes.

More human than his classical antecedents, Proctor is like Willy in his fallibility: they are both guilty of adultery. As the Salem of two hundred years ago seems as far removed as ancient Greece, Miller may endow Proctor with heroic qualities acceptable to a modern audience. At the same time, his human characteristics are all too recognizable. He is impatient with pretense and hypocrisy, and his sharp tongue alienates those whose shortcomings he detects—such as Parris and Putnam. When his reason cannot control his passion for Abby, it ignites action and consequences far beyond his expectations. Through suffering he arrives at the realization that he is responsible both to himself and to his community. In this way his defeat by death is a victory as well.

The Elizabeth of the final scene also has grown in self-awareness through suffering since the tense dinner scene in the second act, when John's reluctance to proclaim the girls' fraud renews Elizabeth's suspicion and provokes John to charge, "You forget nothin' and forgive nothin.'" Sparing in her words throughout the action, Elizabeth in the final scene explains to John the

THE CRUCIBLE

insecurity that drove him into the arms of the "strikingly beautiful," young, and willing Abigail: "I counted myself so plain, so poorly made, no honest love could come to me! Suspicion kissed you when I did; I never knew how I should say my love. It were a cold house I kept!" Her self-recognition leads her to a deeper appreciation of Proctor and his conflicts. She will neither advise nor judge him, but her words, which end the play, indicate, finally, her understanding of him.

While the characters of both Proctor and Elizabeth grow deeper and more complex, Reverend Hale changes radically. On his first entrance, he is described as "an eager-eyed intellectual," sent for as an expert on witchcraft, "finally called upon to face what may be a bloody fight with the Fiend himself." Although Hale prides himself on his expertise, when he first questions Tituba he allows Putnam to insinuate the names of persons she will declare serve the Devil. The actual records of the time indicate that the Putnams and others were motivated more by land envy than by religious conviction. As Miller states in his introductory note, "One could cry witch against one's neighbor and feel perfectly justified in the bargain. . . . suspicions and the envy of the miserable toward the happy could and did burst out in the general revenge."

By the time Hale calls at the Proctors' home in act 2 he is swelling with confidence at his "good work." Despite the proof seen with his own eyes, Hale allows the marshal to take Elizabeth away in chains. Then for the first time a chink appears in the minister's armor of certainty, discernible in gesture rather than in speech: "Hale, in a fever of guilt and uncertainty, turns from the door to avoid the sight."

UNDERSTANDING ARTHUR MILLER

In the third act, when Deputy Governor Danforth refuses to give credence to any testimony counter to his firmly held opinions, Hale's willingness to consider the evidence indicates that he is both more rational and more conscientious. Danforth's reply to Mary's admission of "pretense" is that "four hundred are in the jails from Marblehead to Lynn, and upon my signature" with "seventy-two condemned to hang." He has "not the slightest reason to suspect that the children may be deceiving me." He warns Proctor, "You must understand, sir, that a person is either with this court or he must be counted against it, there be no road between."

Hale asserts, "I am a minister of the Lord, and I dare not take a life without there be a proof so immaculate no slightest qualm of conscience may doubt it." Danforth has no such qualms; he counters that witchcraft is "an invisible crime," so there are no witnesses except the victims, "and they do testify, the children certainly do testify."

Declaring that he believes John and has always suspected Abigail, Hale begs Danforth to "stop now before another is condemned!" He warns that "Private vengeance is working through this testimony!" But Danforth insists that John is lying. Leonard Moss observes that "Proctor is discredited, ironically, because the lie [of Elizabeth] is *believed* . . . while the truth (that Abigail, the adultress, wishes to supplant Elizabeth) is disbelieved."[10] As John is dragged off to jail, Hale finally makes his decision: "I denounce these proceedings, I quit this court!"

In the real-life John Hale's account of the trials, written in 1698 but not published until 1702, after his death, he suspects vengeance as a motive for accusations: "In many of these cases

THE CRUCIBLE

there had been antecedent personal quarrels, and so occasions of revenge; for some of those Condemned, had been suspected by their Neighbours several years, because after quarreling with their Neighbours, evils had befallen those Neighbours."[11]

Abigail Williams's love for John and her desire for respect in the community motivate her "private vengeance" against Elizabeth. In the opening scene Betty charges that in the woods Abigail "drank blood" as "a charm to kill John Proctor's wife!" at which Abigail "smashes her across the face." In the sequence with John which follows, the lure of her sexuality is apparent as well as his struggle to conquer his feelings. Although she is only seventeen now, and the affair has been over for eight months, her love for John is more than physical, as she tearfully declares that he "took me from my sleep and put knowledge in my heart!" "And now," she says, "you bid me tear the light out of my eyes? I will not, I cannot!" An orphan, dependent on her uncle Parris, put out to work, she magnifies the importance of John in her life, the first person ever to treat her as a woman, not as an unwanted dependent or a servant. Her mind exaggerates his feelings for her, the self-esteem she gained by the affair, and her hatred of Elizabeth as the single impediment to a happy future with John. Elizabeth had ended the relationship by dismissing Abigail, "blackening" her name in the village.

When *The Crucible* was staged on Broadway in 1953, Miller says that "the first scene, as the play was originally written, took place in a forest, but this had to be altered because of the expense involved in building this set."[12] During the play's run Miller discarded a distracting set in favor of black drapes and redirected the action, adding a forest scene between John and Abigail. Now part of the published text, as an appendix, it also has appeared as the second scene in act 2.

The added scene reveals more about both Abigail and John. Abigail's opportunism has been evident since the opening scene, when she deflects to Tituba Hale's questions. She is amoral, with no concern for the fate of the good-hearted servant, whom she herself asked for a charm but whom she now denounces as a witch. If Abigail was tough then, by the forest scene she has progressed in her delusions from pretending to actually believing, for the court has elevated her from a dismissed servant to a respected accuser. The change in Abigail is apparent to Proctor, "seeing her madness now," as she tells him, "The jab your wife gave me's not healed yet, y'know," referring to the disproved needle in the poppet. Abigail's newly acquired power is now directed against Elizabeth and all those she believes injured her in the past, with the exception of John, who is "good."

While John's conscience suffers for his adultery and for jeopardizing Elizabeth's life, his guilt can only be intensified by Abby's outburst as she vows, "Oh, John, I will make you such a wife when the world is white again!"

John warns her that, "if you do not free my wife tomorrow, I am set and bound to ruin you, Abby." He tells her he has "rocky proof in documents." For a moment, directs Miller, "wildness stirs in her, a child is standing here who is unutterably frustrated, denied her wish, but she is still grasping for her wits." Her recourse is to cry witchcraft: "They send you! . . . This is your wife pleading, your sniveling, envious wife!" W. David Sievers observes that the scene reveals Abigail's "perverted motives—accusing indiscriminately as she had been accused of looseness.

THE CRUCIBLE

At times she psychotically believes in her own inventions of witchcraft."[13]

John plays his last card: he threatens to reveal their affair. Abigail cannot believe him: "You will confess to fornication? In the court?" He insists, "You will never cry witchery again, or I will make you famous for the whore you are!" As "she wraps herself up as though to go," she also wraps herself in her mad, new identity, believing her illusion: "You have done your duty by her. I hope it is your last hypocrisy." As she leaves, she declares, "Fear naught. I will save you tomorrow. . . . From yourself I will save you. [*She is gone. Proctor is left alone, amazed, in terror.*]"

In the final act Parris reports that Abigail has fled, probably hearing the news that the town of Andover has "thrown out" the court. Opportunistic to the last, she provided for her sea trip by robbing his strongbox. In Miller's screenplay for *The Crucible* (1995) the character of Abigail is considerably enlarged in depicting her hedonistic dancing in the woods, obsession with John, and hysterical "crying out" as well as the town's respect for her as leader of the accusers.

Like all the characters in the play, the devious minister Parris and the covetous landowner Putnam are based on actual persons. Parris's insecurity causes him to ally himself with the authorities and to view the forthright Proctor as an enemy. When Danforth asks his opinion, in act 4, Parris warns: "Let Rebecca stand upon the gibbet and send up some righteous prayer, and I fear she'll wake a vengeance on you." His advice is personal as well as practical: "You cannot hang this sort. There is danger for me. I dare not step outside at night!" From the records, says Miller, "it seems beyond doubt that members of the Putnam family consciously, coldly, and with malice aforethought conferred in private with some of the girls, and told them whom it was desirable to cry out upon next."[14] Giles charges that young Ruth Putnam "named" George Jacobs, prompted by her father, the only man rich enough to buy Jacobs's land, forfeit when he is hanged.

Just as the characters are based on actual persons, yet "creations of my own, drawn . . . in conformity with their known behavior," says the author in his "Note on the Historical Accuracy," so their dialogue is Miller's own invention, yet modeled upon their spoken language, recorded in court and delivered from the pulpit as sermons. It is stark yet eloquent in its simple images and its cadences; it evokes a flavor of seventeenth-century Salem, but it is not a realistic echo; it is Miller's own, artistic version. He reports that, as he sat in Salem's courthouse, reading the town records of 1692, which were "often spelled phonetically . . . [by] the court clerks or the ministers who kept the record as the trials proceeded," he then, "after a few hours of mouthing the words . . . felt a bit encouraged that I might be able to handle it, and in more time I came to love its feel, like hard burnished wood. Without planning to, I even elaborated a few of the grammatical forms myself."[15]

In the language Miller develops from the speech patterns found in the records, the double negative is characteristic. Rebecca Nurse, accused by both Putnams of the deaths of their infants, declares in the court record: "I am innocent and clear. . . . I never afflicted no child. . . . I am as clear [innocent] as the child unborn."[16] Miller also alters the verb conjugations and tenses to conform with those of the period. Intransitive verbs become

transitive—Abby threatens a reckoning that "will shudder you"—
or are transformed to adjectives, as when Mary Warren complains in act 2, on her return from the court, "My insides are all
shuddery." Common verbs, such as *to be* and *to have,* assume a
seventeenth-century flavor: *be* is used for *are* and *am,* as in "be
you foolish?" "I thought it were an auction," complains Proctor
to Parris, describing his sermon urging ownership of his house,
"you spoke so long on deeds and mortgages." With many verbs
present tense indicates the past; *let you* designates the imperative.

Archaic diction is used sparingly, to create an aura of the
past, by choosing simple, familiar words such as *yea* and *nay* and
goodly. Women are addressed as "Goody" instead of "Mrs." In
the quotation cited above, the historical Rebecca uses *clear* to
mean *innocent,* as it does in Shakespeare's plays, but Miller's
Rebecca avoids the archaic word and declares "it is a lie, it is a
lie." Repetition is evocative of the cadences of the Bible, as in
John's first speech: "Be you foolish, Mary Warren? Be you deaf?
I forbid you leave the house, did I not? Why shall I pay you?"
Miller uses strong verbs to create visual imagery: "Leap not to
witchcraft," Parris cautions Putnam in the first act: "They will
howl me out of Salem for such corruption in my home."

The typical rhythm is iambic pentameter, with the stress
falling on monosyllabic words to suggest the strength of characters such as Rebecca, who advises Giles in the opening scene:
"There is hard sickness here . . . so please to keep the quiet."
Miller also uses rhythm and meter poetically, for emotional
effect, as in John's outburst at the end of act 2, presented here as
blank verse in iambic pentameter and hexameter:

> Now Hell and Heaven grapple on our backs,
> And all our old pretense is ripped away. . . .
> We are only what we always were, but naked now. . . .
> Aye, naked! And the wind, God's icy wind, will blow!

As in this passage, nature images often relate to winter, to suggest the harshness of New England life. These lines add divine punishment to extreme suffering and exposure when pretense is stripped away. Abigail reminds John in the opening scene, "You are no wintry man." Stone is an image that recurs in the dialogue, reflecting the actual landscape as well as the hardness of Puritan life. "The devil is precise," says Hale, "the marks of his presence are as definite as stone." Miller wonders at the absence of audience appreciation of this irony. John's final words to Elizabeth are: "Show honor now, show a stony heart and sink them with it!"

In contrast to the images of hardness and of cold and winter are those of heat and fire, for the central metaphor is that of the crucible, in which the heat of fire melts, transforms, and purifies. Omnipresent is the fire of Hell. John's passion for Abigail is described in terms of the "heat" of animals; he confesses to the court in act 3 that his lechery occurred "in the proper place—where my beasts are bedded." In the forest scene (in the play's appendix) Abby uses the image of fire as both purification and passion when she tells Proctor that he "burned away" her ignorance: "It were a fire, John, we lay in fire." In the first scene Ann charges that there are "fires within fires" in the town, while Parris warns that without obedience "the church will burn like Hell is burning!" When John in act 2 agrees to go to Abby, he threatens to "curse her hotter than the oldest cinder in Hell."

THE CRUCIBLE

Some of the burning images relate to working the soil. Farmers burned large stones to make them crack, to which Proctor refers when defending himself to Elizabeth in act 2: "Were I stone I would have cracked for shame this seven month!" That green wood resists fire is alluded to in Hale's remark, "If Rebecca Nurse be tainted, then nothing's left to stop the whole green world from burning." As fire and crucible are central metaphors, the three principals—John, Hale, and Elizabeth—are tested by enduring the fire of suffering which burns away their imperfections, and they emerge as nobler, purer persons.

Images implying good and bad use light and dark and their association with white and black. Name, or reputation, is all-important; Abigail complains that Elizabeth is "blackening" her name in the village. Lucifer's book is "black," as is "mischief." Danforth warns John in act 4 that his "soul alone is the issue here, Mister, and you will prove its whiteness or you cannot live in a Christian country." Abigail in her delusion in the forest scene vows to "scrub the world clean" for the love of God and to make John "such a wife when the world is white again!" Drawing allusions from household duties rings true, for she has been a servant since childhood. One of the most evocative images, based on the simple, everyday act of weaving, appears in John's final speech: "I do think I see some shred of goodness in John Proctor. Not enough to weave a banner with, but white enough to keep it from such dogs."

The color red has traditional associations with murder and passion. A changed Hale appears in the last act, desperate to save the lives of those he himself has condemned. When Danforth inquires why he has returned, he replies: "There is blood on my head! Can you not see the blood on my head!" Abigail, asked by

UNDERSTANDING ARTHUR MILLER

Parris if her name "is entirely white" in the town, replies, "There be no blush about my name." Speaking of generation in the soil, Proctor observes to Elizabeth in act 2, "It's warm as blood beneath the clods," a contrast to the cold and harshness of life on the farm, as is John's appreciation of the flowers and lilacs: "Lilacs have a purple smell. Lilac is the smell of nightfall."

The cadences, rhythms, and even the diction of the Bible enrich Hale's speeches, especially in the final act. As he and Danforth strive to convince John to save his life by admitting a league with the Devil, Danforth's stern threats contrast with Hale's poetic confession: "I came into this village like a bride-groom to his beloved, bearing gifts of high religion; the very crowns of holy law I brought, and what I touched with my bright confidence, it died; and where I turned the eye of my great faith, blood flowed up."

Danforth's imagery is sharp and precise; in act 3 he describes his view of the times with those very words: "This is a sharp time, now, a precise time—we live no longer in the dusky afternoon when evil mixed itself with good and befuddled the world. Now, by God's grace, the shining sun is up, and them that fear not light will surely praise it." Ironically, the night and darkness of the trials will follow his "dusky afternoon." He warns Proctor, "We burn a hot fire here; it melts down all concealment," one of Danforth's many statements with ironic implications, for the concealment of the accusers goes unrecognized, even when Proctor attempts to prove otherwise. The trial as symbol and as dramatic device will reappear in Miller's plays, as will his thesis of acceptance of guilt and responsibility.

THE CRUCIBLE

Gerald Weales asks whether the 1953 play "provide[s] a workable analogy for the American political situation in the early 1950s." He points out that reviewers "accepted it as an immediate political fact" and "supposed that Miller was making specific analogies." But by 1959, notes Weales, "only the lunatic fringe . . . still conceived of *The Crucible* as a *parti pris* political document. It had begun to lead an artistic life of its own." By 1965 Miller was to comment that "McCarthyism may have been the historical occasion of the play, not its theme." Weales believes that "the chief reason why Miller did not go for a one-to-one analogy between the Salem trials and the loyalty hearings of the 1950s is that beyond whatever immediate point he wanted to make as a political man he hoped, as an artist, to create a play that might outlast the moment."[17]

Notes

1. Arthur Miller, *Timebends* (New York: Grove Press, 1987), 331.

2. Ibid., 332, 337.

3. Ibid., 340–41.

4. Ibid., 341.

5. Miller, "Introduction to the *Collected Plays*," in *The Theater Essays of Arthur Miller,* ed. Robert A. Martin (New York: Viking Press, 1978), 154–55.

6. Penelope Curtis, "The Crucible," in *The Crucible: Text and Criticism,* ed. Gerald Weales (New York: Viking Press, 1971), 255–56.

7. "American Bar Association Committee Chairman Sidlo Assails Lines Disparaging Lawyers . . . Miller Refuses to Make Change," *New York Times,* 9 March 1953, sec. 1, p. 3.

8. Miller, "Introduction to the *Collected Plays,*" *Theater Essays,* 158.

9. Robert Hogan, *Arthur Miller* (Minneapolis: University of Minnesota Press, 1964), 28.

10. Leonard Moss, *Arthur Miller* (New York: Twayne, 1967), 62.

11. John Hale, "A Modest Enquiry into the Nature of Witchcraft," in *The Crucible,* ed. Weales 384–85.

12. John and Alice Griffin, "Arthur Miller Discusses *The Crucible,*" *Theatre Arts* 1953 (October): 34.

13. W. David Sievers, "Tennessee Williams and Arthur Miller," *Freud on Broadway* (New York: Cooper Square Publishers, 1955), 398.

14. Miller,"Introduction to the *Collected Plays,*" *Theater Essays,* 157.

15. Miller, *Timebends,* 336.

16. "Records of Salem Witchcraft," in *The Crucible,* ed. Weales, 368–69.

17. Gerald Weales, "Introduction," in *The Crucible,* ed. Weales, xiii–vi.

CHAPTER FIVE

A View from the Bridge

The story of *A View from the Bridge* was told to Arthur Miller by a friend who worked among longshoremen in Red Hook, home of the real-life Eddie Carbone. Miller originally conceived the play in one act in the classical mode: "a hard, telegraphic, unadorned drama" that moved to its catastrophe in a "clear, clean line."[1] Not unlike heroes of Greek tragedy, Carbone is gripped by an overwhelming passion which leads him to a fatal decision: he betrays the social code by which he lives and for which he dies in an attempt to regain his good "name." Lawyer Alfieri is a chorus character who introduces, participates in, and interprets the action, which moves inevitably to a conclusion feared yet anticipated by the audience. As Miller notes, "It must be suspenseful because one knew too well how it would come out, so that the basic feeling would be the desire to stop this man and tell him what he was really doing to his life."[2]

Miller hoped the play would produce the wonderment evoked by Greek tragedies at "the awesomeness of a passion which, despite its contradicting the self-interest of the individual it inhabits, despite every kind of warning, despite even its destruction of the moral beliefs of the individual, proceeds to magnify its power over him until it destroys him."[3] Like some classical heroes and heroines, longshoreman Eddie is gripped by an incestuous sexual passion, here for the niece to whom he has been a father. Unknown and unacknowledged by him, his desire for seventeen-year-old Catherine intensifies when two of his wife's relatives arrive in the country illegally from Sicily. Catherine, who has led a sheltered life, is attracted to and soon falls in love with the younger of the two men, Rodolpho.

When they announce their decision to marry, Eddie's uncontrollable rage and jealousy lead him to break the code of his Sicilian society regarding illegal immigrants. Informing on them to the Immigration Service is a betrayal, punishable by lifelong ostracism, by one's friends, neighbors, and family. As officers lead the brothers away before onlooking neighbors, Marco, the older, points accusingly at Eddie as the informer. In a final fight with Marco, Eddie draws a knife, insisting, "I want my name." The knife is turned against him, and he dies, asking "Why?" The inexorability of events suggested the style to Miller, the "myth-like march of the tale" calling for an unadorned, straightforward fashion, "a fine, high, always visible arc of forces moving in full view to a single explosion."[4]

Miller states that the play was "not designed primarily to draw tears or laughter from an audience" but, rather, to evoke their "astonishment at the way in which, and the reasons for which, a man will endanger and risk and lose his very life."[5] Whether by "distancing" the action to allow the audience to think as well as feel or by directing actors in a realistic rather than a heightened style, the production was judged "cold" by the reviewers when it opened on Broadway in 1955.

Two years later, when director Peter Brook scheduled the London premiere of *A View from the Bridge,* Miller expanded the work to two acts. It is this revised version that is analyzed here, with references to the earlier one-act play as indicated. As Miller explains in the introduction to the revised version, published in

A VIEW FROM THE BRIDGE

1960, Brook's production helped achieve the play's aims: the set, which "soared to the roof with fire escapes [and] passageways, suggested apartments, so that one sensed that Eddie was living out his horror in the midst of a certain normality, and that invisibly . . . he was getting ready to invoke upon himself the wrath of his tribe."

The classically trained British actors, accustomed to playing Shakespeare, easily handled the larger-than-life style the play requires, and the "pay scales of the London theater made it possible to do what I could not do in New York—hire a crowd," reports Miller. When the neighborhood was represented by twenty actors instead of four (Broadway's affordable maximum), the larger group, like a Greek chorus, enhanced the audience's understanding of the main character, says Miller: "the mind of Eddie Carbone is not comprehensible apart from its relation to his neighborhood, his fellow workers, his social situation. His self-esteem depends upon their estimate of him, and his value is created largely by his fidelity to the code of his culture." In the revised version, "once Eddie had been placed squarely in his social context, among his people, the mythlike feeling of the story emerged of itself, and he could be made more human and less a figure, a force," notes Miller.

The chorus character of lawyer Alfieri opens and closes the play. In the two-act version he speaks prose instead of verse, although it is rhythmic, poetic prose. At the beginning Alfieri's cadence also strikes the note of inevitability: "Every few years there is still a case, and as the parties tell me what the trouble is, the flat air in my office suddenly washes in with the green scent of the sea, the dust in this air is blown away and the thought comes that in some Caesar's year . . . another lawyer, quite differently dressed, heard the same complaint and sat there as powerless as I, and watched it run its bloody course. . . . This one's name was Eddie Carbone."

In expanding the play, Miller developed the character of Eddie's wife, Bea, so that she becomes a sympathetic, wronged woman as well as a chorus character less exalted than Alfieri. If he is the voice of society and human nature, she is the voice of the individual neighbors. Another change is the expansion of Catherine's role. The passive recipient of others' attention in the earlier version, she is now active in her own right, a teenager in the flush of first love, anxious to begin a job in the outside world. In the first scene, demurring at the prospect of her working, Eddie finds fault with the neighborhood and the company: "Near the Navy Yard plenty can happen. . . . And a plumbin' company! That's one step over the water front. They're practically long-shoremen." Bea asks: "You gonna keep her in the house all her life?"

At their first meeting with the brothers whom they will harbor, Catherine and Bea are enthusiastic, but Eddie is suspicious, and when blond Rodolpho becomes the center of attention by singing "Paper Doll," Eddie warns him to be quiet: "You don't want to be picked up, do ya?" Helpless in the face of Catherine's obvious attraction to Rodolpho, Eddie tries to undermine him by casting doubt upon his manhood. He complains to Bea in the next scene that the younger man sings at work and is "like a weird." "And with that wacky hair; he's like a chorus girl or sump'm." Eddie consults Alfieri to complain that "the guy ain't right" and to inquire whether there is a law against "a guy which he ain't right can go to work and marry a girl and—?" Eddie's obsession with Catherine increases with the growing threat of Rodolpho, while Bea attempts to avoid an eruption she senses is imminent. In the second scene in act l she asks Eddie, "When am I gonna be a wife again?"

An added scene in act 1 develops the characters of both women. Beatrice cautions her niece: "I told you fifty times already, you can't act the way you act. You still walk around in front of him in your slip." She reminds Catherine tht she is now a grown woman: "You're a woman, that's all, and you got a nice boy, and now the time came when you said good-by. All right?" Catherine is "strangely moved at the prospect." In the parallel scene that follows, Eddie is warned by Alfieri, who is as direct as he can be: "We all love somebody, the wife, the kids—every man's got somebody that he loves, heh? But sometimes . . . there's too much," he cautions, "too much love for the daughter, there is too much love for the niece."

When Alfieri says, "Let her go," Eddie's response leaves no doubt that the obsession is sexual: "I take the blankets off my bed for him, and he takes and puts his dirty filthy hands on her like a goddam thief!" Alfieri replies: "She wants to get married, Eddie. She can't marry you, can she?" Eddie "furiously" charges, "I don't know what the hell you're talkin' about!" Warnings have no effect on Eddie's mounting anger and desperation.

Act 1 concludes on a note of high emotion, as Eddie's oral threats turn physical. Catherine insists on dancing with Rodolpho, whom Eddie, sitting and twisting his newspaper, begins to insult, impugning his manhood. Then his manner changes to cordial. He invites the brothers to a boxing bout, offers to teach Rodolpho, and exchanges a few light blows. Eddie moves in, "feints with his left hand and lands with his right. It mildly staggers Rodolpho." As he and Catherine resume their dancing, Marco challenges Eddie to lift a chair from the bottom of one of its legs, Eddie tries and fails, and Marco "slowly raises the chair higher and higher. . . . like a weapon over Eddie's head—and he transforms what might appear like a glare of warning into a smile of triumph."

The next scene will reach a climax even more intense. Alone in the house with Rodolpho for the first time, Catherine asks if they might live in Italy after they are married: "I'm afraid of Eddie here." Catherine's expanded role reveals her as an active, sympathetic young person in place of the passive object of Bea's and Eddie's wrangling in the first version. She is torn between love for Rodolpho and loyalty to Eddie. Rodolpho urges the weeping girl to make the break and leads her into the bedroom.

As they emerge, Eddie enters, drunk. Eddie orders him out; Catherine says she will go too. Eddie forbids it. "He reaches out suddenly, draws her to him, and as she strives to free herself he kisses her on the mouth." Rodolpho frees her and spins Eddie around. "Rodolpho flies at him in attack. Eddie pins his arms, laughing, and suddenly kisses him." Eddie threatens: "Watch your step, submarine," and warns, "Just get outa here and don't lay another hand on her unless you wanna go out feet first."

Eddie's kissing Catherine confirms his incestuous passion; it is an unguarded act he would never have committed unless both drunk and driven beyond reason by what he perceives to have occurred between her and Rodolpho. It shocks the audience, but even more shocking is his kissing Rodolpho. It culminates Eddie's hints and accusations about Rodolpho's manhood, Eddie's major line of attack. (He also has assured Catherine that the marriage is only to legalize Rodolpho's immigrant status and eligibility for citizenship.)

Have the critics been uncomfortable with this play and especially with this scene? After the initial reviews of both the shorter and longer versions of *A View from the Bridge,* there has been little serious analysis, except for Miller's own comments. Benjamin Nelson feels that there is a "possibility" of "latent homosexuality" in Eddie, because of "his obsession with Rodolpho's 'queerness,' which he attempts to substantiate by humiliating the boy with a savage kiss [that] obviously reveals more about Eddie than about Rodolpho."[6] But this interpretation is unconvincing in the context of Eddie's intensifying sexual obsession with his niece, even to the extent of betraying his community and destroying his own good name.

In a crazed belief that his suspicions have been confirmed by kissing Rodolpho, Eddie pays a last visit to Alfieri, who is dubious: "You didn't prove anything about him. It sounds like he just wasn't strong enough to break your grip." The lawyer warns him that "the law is nature. The law is only a word for what has a right to happen. . . . Let her go." As Eddie leaves, Alfieri suspects that, to destroy Rodolpho, Eddie will even destroy himself.

Alfieri voices the apprehension and fears of the audience about the catastrophe that is to ensue. Eddie phones the Immigration Bureau and informs on Rodolpho and Marco. "The betrayal achieves its true proportions as it flies in the face of the mores administered by Eddie's conscience—which is also the conscience of his friends, co-workers, and neighbors," notes Miller.[7]

Like Oedipus, Eddie will be thrust from the community for an act that harms it. He also resembles John Proctor in his determination to preserve his good name at any cost, even death. A climactic scene closes the play. Having spit in Eddie's face and denounced him in front of the neighbors, Marco returns. He and Eddie both seek the final encounter. Eddie rejects Rodolpho's apology and insists that he wants his "name," which Marco took from him. Beatrice attempts to bar Eddie's way and cries out the truth: "You want somethin' else, Eddie, and you can never have her!"

To the surrounding neighbors, Eddie attempts to justify himself as one wronged by strangers he sheltered: "to come out of the water and grab a girl for a passport? . . . Wipin' the neighborhood with my name like a dirty rag! I want my name, Marco." He attacks Marco, who strikes him; Eddie goes down, then springs a knife and lunges with it, but Marco turns the blade back to him and presses it as Eddie falls to his knees. He dies in Beatrice's arms, and Alfieri steps from the crowd to speak the final words:

> Most of the time now we settle for half and I like it better. But the truth is holy, and even as I know how wrong he was, and his death useless, I tremble, for I confess that something perversely pure calls to me from his memory—not purely good, but himself purely, for he allowed himself to be wholly known and for that I think I will love him more than all my sensible clients. And yet, it is better to settle for half, it must be! And so I mourn him—I admit it—with a certain . . . alarm.

A VIEW FROM THE BRIDGE

A View from the Bridge is a tragedy of the common man, as defined by Miller, in which the hero, regardless of his station in life, is totally compelled "to evaluate himself justly." Eddie, like Willy Loman, is unwilling "to remain passive in the face of what he conceives to be a challenge to his dignity, his image of his rightful status." Miller notes that "the commonest of men may take on . . . [tragic] stature to the extent of his willingness to throw all he has into the contest, the battle to secure his rightful place in his world." His plight evokes fear in the audience, "fear of being displaced, the disaster inherent in being torn away from our chosen image of what and who we are in this world."[8]

As Miller explains in his introduction to the two-act version, the expanded *View from the Bridge* enabled him to include "the viewpoint of Eddie's wife, and *her* dilemma in relation to him." Making Beatrice active rather than passive deepens her portrayal as well as that of Eddie. Now a strong character, Bea is, however, helpless in the face of impending disaster, although her accusations and warnings shed additional light on Eddie's character. When she challenges him about Rodolpho—"what you done to him in front of her"—Eddie insists: "A wife is supposed to believe the husband. If I tell you that guy ain't right don't tell me he is right."

In a new scene with Beatrice in act 2, after phoning the Immigration Bureau, Eddie reveals his insecurity, even his fear that he is losing his accustomed control over the family. Now it is Beatrice, not the brothers, making the decision that they should move upstairs. Eddie's response, "wanting to beat down her evident disapproval of him," is: "I got a couple of rights here. This is my house here not their house."

As Eddie dies in the revised final scene, there is another change in his relationship with Beatrice. In the original version, after Eddie is fatally wounded, "he crawls a yard to Catherine. ... he reaches over and grasps her leg, and, looking up at her, he seems puzzled, questioning, betrayed." Eddie asks, "Catherine—why—?" as Catherine "covers her face and weeps. She sinks down beside the weeping Beatrice," who is not reconciled with Eddie. In the revised version both women support Eddie as he "falls to his knees before Marco." Catherine tells him, "Eddie I never meant to do nothing bad to you."

EDDIE: Then why—Oh, B.!
BEATRICE: Yes, yes!
EDDIE: My B.! [*He dies in her arms, and* BEATRICE *covers him with her body.*]

Robert Hogan observes, "this reconciliation with his wife perhaps normalizes Eddie more, but it also lessens his stature."[9] It would seem that, if his fatal obsession for Catherine so dominates Eddie that he has risked everything, he might well turn to her as he dies, still seeking an explanation. On the other hand, in the revised version Eddie in his final moments may be realizing the truth he denied in life and turning to Bea for forgiveness.

Miller also changes Alfieri's final speech. In the original version he was more lyric. As he did in his introduction, Alfieri at the close links the events just witnessed with those of the past, "Leading back toward some ancestral beach / Where all of us once lived." Although in the expanded version Alfieri's lines are

A VIEW FROM THE BRIDGE

set as prose, they are frequently as poetic as those in the one-act, where they are set as free verse. In the revised version, in lyrical prose, Alfieri creates the scene: "But this is Red Hook, not Sicily. This is the slum that faces the bay on the seaward side of Brooklyn Bridge. This is the gullet of New York swallowing the tonnage of the world." Miller's added alliteration and metaphor lift Alfieri's comments to a poetic level and contrast it to the action's realistic dialogue. Rodolpho's paean to motorcycles shortly after his entrance is set as verse in the one-act version. In the revision the identical speech in prose format has a lyrical quality, whereas it seems prosaic when set as verse.

Miller again meets the challenge to create dialogue that is convincingly realistic and at the same time heightened and poetic. Unlike *The Crucible,* in which he invented a virtually new language for his seventeenth-century characters, here his people, except for Alfieri, are uneducated longshoremen and their families. To express emotions on a scale that is larger than life, Miller gives them speech that is zestful, rhythmic, and unadorned. Verbs are active and adjectives simple, with little imagery except for everyday allusions. Descriptions are vivid and direct, as in Beatrice's account, early in the action, of a teenaged informer: "He had five brothers and the old father. And they grabbed him in the kitchen and pulled him down the stairs—three flights his head was bouncin' like a coconut."

Omissions, double negatives, irregular syntax, and other ungrammatical constructions achieve effects that are realistic and at times humorous. When Catherine in act 1 announces a job offer, Eddie is at first resentful, then reluctantly agrees and offers advice:

EDDIE: I only ask you one thing—don't trust nobody.
You got a good aunt but she's got too big a heart, you
learned bad from her. Believe me.

BEATRICE: Be the way you are, Katie, don't listen to him.

EDDIE: [*to* BEATRICE—*strangely and quickly resentful*]
You lived in a house all your life, what do you know about
it? You never worked in your life.

BEATRICE: She likes people. What's wrong with that?

EDDIE: Because most people ain't people.

While the speech of the longshoremen and their families
sounds contemporary, Alfieri's poetic passages evoke the past
with musical, alliterative proper names: "some Caesar's year, in
Calabria perhaps or on the cliff at Syracuse." The Brooklyn
Bridge is symbolic, as Nada Zeineddine notes, "as a link between
modern Brooklyn and traditional Sicily—a bridge between the
past and the present."[10] The "view" of the title suggests an
objective distancing between the action and the view of it by
Alfieri and the audience.

Although Miller notes that he had been carrying the story
around in his head for a long time, he wrote the play's first version
in ten days, when asked by an actors' group for a one-act play to
present (along with *A Memory of Two Mondays*) in their theater,
unused on Sundays. When the actors' play closed, he agreed to
a production on Broadway. But the reviews were disappointing:
"If *A View from the Bridge* more than thirty years later has a
vigorous life on stages all over the world, it is no thanks to the
original production, which made it appear at best an academic
and irrelevant story of revenge," says Miller. "What I had written
was something very different, something plain and elementary

and frightening in its inexorability. . . . the play on the stage had no tang; it lacked the indefinable webbing of human involvment that can magically unify many otherwise dismally ordinary separate parts."[11]

Two years later the British premiere of the expanded play was a great success. Miller writes of Eddie in this production's two-act version: "The importance of his interior psychological dilemma was magnified. . . . What had seemed like a mere aberration had now risen to a fatal violation of an ancient law." He concludes, "It is more possible now to relate his actions to our own and thus to understand ourselves a little better not only as isolated psychological entities, but as we connect to our fellows and our long past together."[12]

Notes

1. Arthur Miller, "Introduction," *A View from the Bridge: A Play in Two Acts* (New York: Viking Press, 1960), vi.

2. Ibid., vii.

3. Arthur Miller, "Introduction to the *Collected Plays,*" in *The Theater Essays of Arthur Miller,* ed. Robert A. Martin (New York: Viking Press, 1978), 163.

4. Arthur Miller, "On Social Plays," *A View from the Bridge: Two One-Act Plays* (New York: Viking Press, 1955), 17.

5. Ibid., 18.

6. Benjamin Nelson, *Arthur Miller* (London: Peter Owen, 1970), 214.

7. Miller, "Introduction to the *Collected Plays,*" *Theater Essays,* 167.

8. Arthur Miller, "Tragedy and the Common Man," *Theater Essays,* 4–6.

9. Robert Hogan, *Arthur Miller* (Minneapolis: University of Minnesota Press, 1964), 35.

10. Nada Zeineddine, *Because It Is My Name* (Braunton, Devon, U.K.: Merlin Books, 1991), 181.

11. Arthur Miller, *Timebends* (New York: Grove Press, 1987), 354–55.

12. Miller, "Introduction," *A View from the Bridge,* ix–x.

CHAPTER SIX

Two Plays of the Depression

A Memory of Two Mondays and *The American Clock*

Arthur Miller writes from experience about the Depression: "through no fault or effort of mine it was the ground upon which I learned to stand." He began writing plays "in the midst of what Allan Seager . . . calls one of the two genuinely national catastrophes in American history—the Great Depression of the thirties. The other was the Civil War."[1] Although today the period is viewed with some "romanticism," it was actually "a terribly frustrating time, when the least thing one wished to do was impossible because there was no money," but it was also a "strong" time, "a common experience when everybody was in the same boat, and perhaps we understood each other a little better then," the author commented in introducing a 1970 National Educational Television version of *A Memory of Two Mondays*.

Miller describes this play as "a pathetic comedy; a boy works among people for a couple of years, shares their troubles, their victories, their hopes, and when it is time for him to be on his way he expects some memorable moment, some sign from them that he has been among them, that he has touched them and been touched by them. In the sea of routine that swells around them they barely note his departure." It was written, he states in the introduction to the *Collected Plays,* "in part out of a desire to relive a sort of reality where necessity was open and bare; I hoped to define for myself the value of hope, why it must arise, as well as the heroism of those who know, at least, how to endure its

UNDERSTANDING ARTHUR MILLER

absence. Nothing in this book was written with greater love, and for myself I love nothing printed here better than this play."[2]

The play, which compacts Miller's memories of several years as a stock boy in an auto parts warehouse, "tries to set the mood and the nature of the times, for at least one young fellow who was on his way elsewhere, passing through this box, this warehouse, where these people are caught, caught by necessity and by their lives." In his introduction to the television version he observed that the dusty warehouse, cold in winter and hot in summer, along with the "endless days of work, five and a half days a week for a pittance," may seem "awful" to viewers today, but it was "a haven in the thirties. It was a place to go; at least you had a job—this was a great thing—that's what remained with me—that I was so lucky."

In the printed text Miller observes that the warehouse setting, although "dirty and unmanageably chaotic," is also "a little world, a home to which, unbelievably perhaps, these people like to come every Monday morning, despite what they say." The two Mondays of the title are a Monday morning in summer when young Bert is just beginning his job as a warehouse stockboy, and a winter Monday when Bert is about to leave for college, having saved the five hundred dollars' tuition out of his weekly salary. The people of the "little world" of the warehouse, as seen through Bert's eyes, are brought vividly to life. The mood is nostalgic, even elegiac at times, like Gus's recounting his years at the warehouse in terms of bygone automobiles.

There is a story rather than a plot, notes Miller. The story is a simple one: Bert acts and interacts with his fellow employees, and at the end he leaves while they remain. All the action takes place in "the shipping room of a large auto-parts warehouse" with

TWO PLAYS OF THE DEPRESSION

a long packing table and "factory-type windows which reach from floor to ceiling and are encrusted with the hard dirt of years." In this setting "the men take orders off the hook, go out into the bin-lined alleys, fill the orders, bring the merchandise back to the table, where Kenneth packs and addresses everything."

The main characters include three middle-aged men: Raymond, who has worked his way up to the position of manager; Larry, who is still a clerk in need of a raise to support his family; and Tom, the accountant who is almost fired for drunkenness the first Monday but who, by the second, has beaten the habit. About the same age is the boss, Mr. Eagle, who passes through the area only on his way to the toilet but whose approach heralds instant animation among the workers as well as attempts to shield absent or incapacitated fellow employees. The two older men are sixty-eight-year-old Gus, who is Slavic and tough, and his pal Jim, an Indian fighter out West "up to McKinley"; he denies being a hundred years old, confessing to seventy-six. The principal younger men are Bert, who is eighteen (Miller's age in 1933), and Kenneth, a young Irish immigrant who sings and recites poetry. There are two women, Agnes the switchboard operator, described as "a spinster in her late forties, always on the verge of laughter," and Patricia, twenty-three, "blankly pretty" and "not quite sure who she is yet."

Gus is the most colorful and the most memorable of the employees, although each has an area of expertise which Bert admires. Gruff and outspoken, Gus wears a bowler hat in the office and on his first appearance is "not completely sober, not bright yet," for he and Jim have just spent the weekend in carousing and heavy drinking. Gus's wife, Lilly, is incurably ill; he telephones her but hangs up in disgust when "she don't hear nothing." He, like Agnes, is protective of the drunken Tom. Fearing Tom will be fired, Gus threatens to go as well: "You fire Tommy, you fire me!" At the end of the first Monday comes the news that Gus's wife has died. By the second Monday, in winter, he has changed; he has never recovered from the death of Lilly, whom he left to die alone while he was drunk in Staten Island.

When Gus receives her insurance money of five thousand dollars, he goes on a spectacular binge with Jim; on the second Monday they arrive at work drunk, in new clothes, carrying two fenders for his new car, which he has wrecked. He is unthreatened by Mr. Eagle's imminent arrival. In an elegiac tribute to times gone by, Gus sums up, in a catalog of cars now extinct, his twenty-two years at the warehouse: "When there was Winton Six I was here. When was Minerva car I was here. When was Stanley Steamer I was here, and Stearns Knight, and Marmon was good car; I was here all them times. . . . When was Locomobile, and Model K Ford and Model N Ford—all them different Fords, and Franklin was good car, Jordan car, Reo car, Pierce Arrow, Cleveland car—all them was good cars. All them times I was here."

He and Jim walk out, even though it is only nine-thirty in the morning. At lunchtime the next day, Bert's last, Jim relates that, on one last spree, Gus has died. "I'm gonna do it right," Gus kept repeating. He spent all the money, riding in different cabs after they lost the car. With Gus in one cab, Jim in another, and a third cab to follow in case of a flat tire, they went to "some real high-class places," and Gus telephoned friends and family all over the country. When the cabs stopped at a light, Jim went up to Gus's cab, opened the door, "and he—was dead. Right there in the seat. It was just gettin' to be morning."

TWO PLAYS OF THE DEPRESSION

Although with one final fling Gus at last breaks the monotony of long years of work, all the others are more cautious. They need their jobs. Larry, "a troubled but phlegmatic man," knows where every auto part is stored in the entire five-story warehouse. He is the father of triplets, and even though he is refused a five-dollar a week raise, he defiantly buys an Auburn car because "they've got the most beautifully laid-out valves in the country on that car, and I want it, that's all." Possessing it even earns him some attention from Patricia, the office beauty. But by the second Monday he has had to sell the Auburn: "It's out of my class anyway." His romance with Patricia has come to an end as well.

Within the space of ninety minutes Miller manages to make his viewers and readers care about the characters, each of whom is an individual, even though the workplace and the frustrations are the same. Yet, Bert reflects in a verse soliloquy, they all stay:

> How is it me that gets out?
> I don't know half the poems Kenneth does,
> Or a quarter of what Larry knows about an engine.
> I don't understand how they come every morning,
> Every morning and every morning,
> And no end in sight.
> That's the thing—there's no end!
> Oh, there ought to be a statue in the park—
> "To All the Ones That Stay."
> One to Larry, to Agnes, Tom Kelly, Gus . . .

Kenneth, who only recently has arrived from Ireland and is nearest Bert in age, evokes the most pathos in this "pathetic comedy." Singing and reciting poetry, he replies, when Bert asks how he learned it all, "Why, in Ireland, Bert; there's all kinds of useless occupations in Ireland." Some of his dialogue, like Bert's, is in free verse, but even his prose speeches are poetic: "It's the poetry hour, Gus," he announces. "This is the hour all men rise to thank God for the blue of the sky, the roundness of the everlasting globe, and the cheerful cleanliness of the subway system. And here we have some axles. Oh, Bert, I never thought I would end me life wrappin' brown paper around strange axles."

Kenneth wonders to Gus whether Bert is "only kiddin'" about going to college someday: "I suppose he's just got some strong idea in his mind. That's the thing, y'know. I often conceive them myself, but I'm all the time losin' them, though."

While inertia seems to grip the others, Kenneth, after only a few months there, is still full of energy. He decides, with Bert's help, to wash the dirt-encrusted windows, which reach from floor to ceiling. As they do so, Miller signals the passage of time: "they make one slow swipe of the window before them and instantly all the windows around the stage burst into the yellow light of summer that floods into the room." Then the changing of the seasons is conveyed by the verse dialogue of the young men: "a real summer sky and a little white cloud goin' over," "the leaves falling on the gray days," a tree "turning red," and "Don't cats walk dainty in the snow!" *"Gradually, as they speak, all light hardens to that of winter, finally."*

By the second Monday, in winter, Kenneth is disillusioned with life; he has forgotten his poetry, lost his optimism, and turned to drink. About to depart for college, Bert suggests that Kenneth, being smarter than he is, could learn anything. Kenneth replies, *"his manner . . . rougher, angrier, less careful of proprieties":*

TWO PLAYS OF THE DEPRESSION

> How's a man to live,
> Freezing all day in this palace of dust
> And night comes with one window and a bed
> And the streets full of strangers
> And not one of them's read a book through,
> Or seen a poem from beginning to end
> Or knows a song worth singing.
> Oh, this is an ice-cold city, Mother,
> And Roosevelt's not makin' it warmer, somehow.

Throughout the action Kenneth sings the Irish ballad "The Minstrel Boy," symbolic of both himself and Bert. Although, like the minstrel boy, Kenneth has hope and optimism at first, he has lost these by the second Monday. He has thoughts of joining the Civil Service, but, he tells Bert, "I've a feelin' I'd never dare leave it, y'know? And I'm not ready for me last job yet, I think. I don't want nothin' to be the last, yet." Even this hope dims when, in his drunkenness, he has thrown over a bar and will have to pay for all the ruined liquor and glasses.

The ending is poignant, when Bert departs from companions of long days together, who now hardly seem to notice. Bert reflects that he will remember them always

> And still I know that in a month or two
> They'll forget my name, and mix me up
> With another boy who worked here once,
> And went.

Bert at least is "on his way elsewhere, passing through," while the others are "caught by necessity and by their lives." Like the minstrel boy in Kenneth's song, which concludes the play, Bert sets out for the war of life, wearing a "wild harp slung behind him."

There is humor as well as pathos in this "pathetic comedy." A point Miller consistently makes about the Depression is that, despite difficulties, people had spirit; they could laugh and joke about the hard times as well as lament them. The physical humor in *A Memory of Two Mondays* springs naturally from the situations. Gus is so outrageously larger than life that everything he does is in the realm of hyperbole, rising to a climax in the final spree, as described by Jim. Even though Gus cynically disparages the hopes of his fellow workers, he is always good-natured. The reactions of the workers are both humorous and characteristic when Bert's and Kenneth's washing of windows "encrusted with the hard dirt of years" discloses a next-door bordello.

In a brief cameo in which a mechanic seeks an obsolete part for his ancient truck, the dialogue exemplifies Miller's distinctive gift for speech that is humorous in its content, poetic in its rhythm, and realistic in its detail: "a very old coal truck, see, and I thought it was a Mack . . . on the engine it says American LaFrance." He doesn't know the year of the truck, although an old man told him that "when he was a boy already that truck was an old truck, and he's an old, old man, that guy." Bert is instructed to find the part amid Model T mufflers and Maxwell differentials. It recalls a time when the worn-out was not discarded but, instead, valued and repaired over and over again.

Drinking seems to be the one escape shared by the employees—not only Gus and Jim but also Tom and, in the second half, Kenneth. That they are or become drunkards is not an exaggeration. Miller relates in *Timebends* that he breaks in as his replacement a young man "fresh off the boat, a young giant with a lovely brogue" who "was soon struggling against becoming a drunk, as most of them had had to do at some time in their working lives, understandably, I thought, given that they knew there was absolutely no future for them here and at the same time that they had to be thankful for working at all in those days. The repression of anger, though, was not always successful."[3]

Not only was *A Memory of Two Mondays* coolly received by the reviewers when it opened on Broadway in 1955; some of them failed to mention it all, devoting their space to criticizing the one-act version of *A View from the Bridge,* with which it shared the evening. Miller believes that in New York in 1955 with the stock market rising and the dollar the world's currency, "a play about workers was the last thing anybody wanted to think about." When produced abroad, however, the play "made a mark for itself—in Latin America, Italy, Czechoslovakia, and the less affluent countries of Europe which still had such workers and conditions of work or could remember them."[4]

Thirty-one years later Miller's second play about the Depression, *The American Clock,* also would be more appreciated abroad. Described by Miller as "a 'mural' of American society in the Depression crisis," he realized too late that "the very word *society* is death on Broadway." In the early 1970s the play was given a lackluster production, incorporating many revisions demanded by the producer, who persuaded Miller "to personalize what should have been allowed its original epic impulse, its concentration on the collapse of a society." A few days after opening, playing to nearly full theater capacity, it had to close, because the producer had no money left with which to advertise, "such was the brutal inanity of Broadway."[5]

At London's National Theatre in 1986 *The American Clock* fared much better. Miller describes the play as "a vaudeville," with dramatic scenes set in the towns and farmlands of America and period songs sung by a chorus to an onstage jazz band. As in vaudeville, the dramatic sketches are brief and interspersed among song-and-dance numbers. Paralleling Miller's account of his boyhood in *Timebends* is a continuing family saga. When the play begins in 1929 Moe Baum loses his money and his manufacturing business in the crash; he and his wife, Rose, and son, Lee, must leave their luxurious New York apartment and go to live in a small house in Brooklyn, as did the Millers. Moe becomes a salesman, Rose pawns her jewelry, and Lee gives up hopes of entering college.

Based on Studs Terkel's *Hard Times,* a 1970 book of interviews with survivors of the Depression, the short sketches form a panorama depicting every level of society. Some of the participants, and many who are alluded to, are from real life. Theodore K. Quinn, singing "Million-Dollar Baby," opens the play. A neighbor of Miller's, Quinn worked himself up from a poor law student to vice president and then president of General Electric, an office he held for one day, at the end of which he resigned, fearing that monopolies like the one he had created might ruin America's "free, competitive economy and the political liberties it makes possible." Quinn loved soft-shoe dancing: "As Quinn agonizes over whether to accept the presidency of GE, a phone rings at the edge of the stage; plainly it is as the new president that he must answer it. He taps his way over to it, lifts the receiver, and simply places it gently on the floor and dances joyously away." Miller notes, "In this antic yet thematically precise spirit, accompanied by some forty songs out of the period, the show managed to convey the *seriousness* of the disaster that the Great Depression was, and at the same time its human heart."[6]

The rapid-fire succession of scenes reflects the swiftness with which the bad news of the crash spread. Stunned financiers sit at a bar describing a colleague's fall from a window, followed by Moe firing his chauffeur, Frank. Frank protests that he has nowhere to go except to live with in-laws "I never got along with" and walks off, as Irene, a middle-aged black woman, waltzes in singing, picks up the discarded lap robe, and comments: "You got fired, you walked away to nothing; no unemployment insurance, no Social Security—just the in-laws and fresh air."

A member of the chorus who also narrates and plays a role is Arthur A. Robertson, a financier who anticipated the crash; he outwitted the bank failures by carrying his money in his shoes. After witnessing a riotous farm auction that leads to a near-lynching, he comments: "Nobody knows how many people are leaving their hometowns, their farms and cities, and hitting the road. Hundreds of thousands, maybe millions of internal refugees, Americans transformed into strangers."

One of the farmers turns up later at the Baum house, homeless, fainting from hunger, asking to work for food and a bed in the basement. Asked the identity of the drifter, Moe replies: "He's a farmer from Iowa. He tried to lynch a judge, so she wanted him to live in the cellar."

After many jobs and much saving, Lee has managed, near the end of the play, to enter college: "Two pairs of socks and a shirt, plus a good shirt and a mackinaw, and maybe a part-time job in the library, and you could live like a king and never see cash. So there was a distinct reluctance to graduate," especially into a world "where you knew nobody wanted you."

Despite the darkness of the days, the period songs sung by Lee and his mother, by Quinn, and by the chorus are always hopeful and joyous, such as "Sunny Side of the Street." A scene in the welfare office, the suicide of Joey, a dentist selling flowers in the subway, a Mississippi sheriff bullying a black cook, all depict some of the more threatening aspects of the times. The irony is intentional, notes Miller: "the play should have the swift panache of vaudeville, a smiling and extroverted style, in itself an irony when the thematic question was whether America, like all civilizations, had a clock running on it, an approaching time of weakening and death." He explains to Peter Wood, director of the British production, that "at the play's end . . . we should feel, along with the textures of a massive social and human tragedy, a renewed awareness of the American's improvisational strength, his almost subliminal faith that things can and must be made to work out."[7]

The title, as Miller indicates, is symbolic. One characteristic of the period especially lent itself to dramatic interpretation: "the introduction into the American psyche of a certain unprecedented *suspense*. Through the twenties the country . . . floated in a reassuring state of nature that merged boundlessly with the sea and the sky."[8] The characters at the very beginning of the play reflect this confidence, like shoeshiner Clarence, who rejects Robertson's advice to sell all his stocks, because Andrew Mellon predicts the market will continue to rise. "But the Crash," Miller

TWO PLAYS OF THE DEPRESSION

observes, "forced us all to enter history willy-nilly, and everyone soon understood that there were other ways of conducting the nation's business—there simply had to be, because the one we had was so persistently not working. It was not only the radicals who were looking at the historical clock and asking how long our system could last, but people of every viewpoint."[9]

Suspense pervades the final family scene. The windows shut tight on a suffocating July day, Rose is playing cards with her sister and her niece. She is fearfully awaiting an eviction notice served by a "professional collector" who is "merciless." Studying their cards, "the women freeze," as Rose, "isolated in light," speaks to the audience about the rotogravure heroes she admired, such as President Warren Gamaliel Harding and Mayor James J. Walker who "smiled like an angel, what a nose, and those tiny feet. Richard Whitney, president of the Stock Exchange. . . . Who could know that these upright handsome men would either turn out to be crooks who would land in jail or ignoramuses? What is left to believe? The bathroom. I lock myself in and hold on to the faucets so I shouldn't scream."

The suspense continues. Moe arrives home "nearly beaten," having sold nothing. There is a persistent knocking at the door, as Rose prays: "God in heaven . . . make him go away!" She continues: "give Mr. Roosevelt the way to help us . . . [*Door knock.*] Oh, my God, help our dear country . . . and the people! . . . *Door knock. Fadeout.*"

The last sequence takes place years later. Lee is a sports reporter, his songwriting cousin Sidney a security guard. They reminisce about friends who died in World War II, Korea, and Vietnam. In a reprise of their first scene Rose, resurrected, and

Lee sing "Life Is Just a Bowl of Cherries," and the company "takes up the song in a soft, long-lost tonality." The final words are spoken by Robertson and Quinn over the singing. Quinn claims, "Roosevelt saved them," to which Robertson counters, "Up to a point; but what really got us out of it was the war." Quinn replies: "Roosevelt gave them back their belief in the country. The government belonged to them again! . . . The return of that belief is what saved the United States, no more, no less!"

> ROBERTSON: I think that's putting it a little too . . .
> QUINN: [*cutting him off and throwing up his hands*]
> That's it! . . . God, how I love that music! [*He breaks into his soft-shoe dance as the singing grows louder. He gestures for the audience to join in, and the company does so as well as the chorus swells . . .*]END

Because the aims of this "vaudeville" are elsewhere, Rose is the only fully developed character. She is a true original, breathing life and humanity into the family sequences, in contrast to the panorama of forty-three other speaking roles depicting American society during the Depression. In the opening family scene the light rises on Rose at the piano, "dressed for an evening out," singing with Lee, instructing him to "breathe," and proudly commenting: "Rudy Vallee is turning green." Moe phones his broker, the chauffeur arrives, and the parents depart, Rose in furs. In her next appearance she is pawning her jewelry; soon the family, including her father, are living in Brooklyn. She is making the best of the move to a small house: "Still . . . it was very nice in a certain way. On our block in Brooklyn a lot of married children had to move back with the parents, and you heard babies crying in houses that didn't have a baby in twenty years. But of course the doubling up could also drive you crazy."

During the scenes of the family's tribulations what keeps them going is Rose's "improvisational strength," what Miller views as a particularly American response to the Depression. The very fact that she can alter her outlook, although it puzzles Lee, is a saving grace for her and her family. As Moe and Lee leave for work at the end of act 1, she assures her husband, "This is going to be a good day—I know it!" Handing Lee his lunch bag, she asserts, "And listen—it doesn't mean you can *never* go to college." Lee catches her optimism: "Oh, I don't mind, Ma," adding, "I'm lucky I got the job!" He is the only wage earner, as Moe is selling ladies' lingerie on commission of a tenth of a cent on each item.

In a poignant exchange Moe asks Lee to lend him a quarter for subway fare and a hotdog. Lee addresses the audience: "it was hard to look at one another. So we pretended nothing had happened. . . . But something had. . . .It was like I'd started to support my *father!* And why that should have made me feel so happy, I don't know, but it did!"

From Miller's autobiography it can be surmised that his own mother was the inspiration for Rose. Augusta Miller was a cultured woman who played the piano and sang, read extensively, and deplored the fact that she was married off by her parents before she could attend college. Rose complains to Lee, "They treat a woman like a cow, fill her up with a baby and lock her in for the rest of her life."

Rose's good humor in the face of adversity gives the family strength to endure. She recognizes the incongruity between their aspirations and the reality that thwarts them. Act 2 begins with

Rose singing at the piano while musing between bars, "Wherever you look there's a contest; Kellogg's, Post Toasties, win five thousand, win ten thousand. I guess I ought to try, but the winners are always in Indiana somehow."

Perceptive and sensitive to her surroundings, she is an ideal observer of the details with which Miller paints his picture of life in the Depression: "There's a dozen college graduates with advanced degrees playing ball in the street like children." Their neighbor, Mr. Warsaw, "to make a little money he started a racetrack in his kitchen, with cockroaches. Keeps them in match-boxes with their names written on—Alvin, Murray, Irving . . . They bet nickels, dimes." Illness was a real fear: "I only pray to God our health holds up, because one filling and you've got to lower the thermostat for a month."

Devoted to her music, playing Schumann as well as Gershwin, Rose declares: "This piano is not leaving this house. Jewelry, yes, but nobody hocks this dear, darling piano." She is a reader: "I must go to the library—I must start taking out some good books again; I must stop getting so stupid." Another of Rose's practices that Miller relates about his own mother in the Depression is feeding the homeless, one of whom moves in with them.

But even Rose, with her warmheartedness, her optimism, and her humor, is eventually worn down by the unrelenting hard times. She is near a breakdown in the card-playing scene in which she dreads the eviction server. When her relatives suggest that Moe might ask his wealthy mother for help, Rose bitterly replies: "His mother says there's a Depression going on." She concludes, "The next time I start believing in anybody or anything I hope my tongue is cut out!" She screams and weeps at her husband when he returns home penniless and challenges him to "go to your mother and stand up like a man to her . . . instead of this goddamned fool!" The scene and the saga of the Baum family ends with Rose and Moe nearly frozen with fear, as the knocking at the door continues.

At the end Lee's epitaph for his mother epitomizes her vital character and reveals his understanding. Rose appears as a ghostly presence and sings as Lee speaks:

> After all these years I still can't settle with myself about my mother. In her own crazy way she was so much like the country. . . . There was nothing she believed that she didn't also believe the opposite. . . . She'd lament her fate as a woman. . . . but then she'd warn me, "Watch out for women—when they're not stupid, they're full of deceit." I'd come home and give her a real bath of radical idealism, and she was ready to storm the barricades; by evening she'd fallen in love again with the Prince of Wales. She was so like the country. . . . With all her defeats she believed to the end that the world was meant to be better. . . . I don't know; all I know for sure is that whenever I think of her, I always end up—with this headful of life!

Notes

1. Arthur Miller, "The Shadows of the Gods," in *The Theater Essays of Arthur Miller,* ed. Robert A. Martin (New York: Viking Press, 1978), 176.

2. Arthur Miller, "Introduction to the *Collected Plays,*" *Theater Essays,* 163–64.

3. Arthur Miller, *Timebends* (New York: Grove Press, 1987), 219.

4. Ibid., 220.

5. Ibid., 586–87.

6. Arthur Miller, "Introduction," *The American Clock* (New York: Grove Press, 1989), xviii– xix.

7. Miller, *Timebends,* 588.

8. Miller, "Introduction," *The American Clock,* xiii.

9. Ibid.

CHAPTER SEVEN

After the Fall
and *Incident at Vichy*

After the Fall

None of Arthur Miller's plays was anticipated with higher expectations or greeted with more vilification than *After the Fall.* Absent from the Broadway stage for nine years, Miller by 1964 was a major American playwright. When it was announced that his new play would inaugurate the repertory theater of the new Lincoln Center for the Performing Arts and that in its opening week the play would be published in the *Saturday Evening Post,* excitement reached fever proportions. New York City newsstands sold out of the *Post* the day it appeared; papers reported almost daily on the progress of the temporary building on West Fourth Street and on the acting company housed there while Lincoln Center was under construction.

When *After the Fall* opened, rage rather than critical evaluation was the reviewers' response. Robert Brustein wrote: "Mr. Miller is dancing a spiritual striptease while the band plays mea culpa. . . . He has created a shameless piece of tabloid gossip, an act of exhibitionism which makes us all voyeurs."[1] While some critics saw only "the most nakedly autobiographical drama ever put on public view," Miller protested that the "man up there isn't me . . . a playwright doesn't put himself on the stage, he only dramatizes certain forces within himself."[2] The play's dramatic and philosophical worth went virtually unnoticed, while angry reactions focused upon the marriage of the hero, Quentin, to a popular sex symbol named Maggie. It was impossible not to recognize the resemblance to Miller's much-publicized romance with and marriage to movie star Marilyn Monroe, followed by divorce and her suicide by an overdose of sleeping pills. That the actress playing Maggie (a singing star in the play) was directed by Elia Kazan to wear a bouffant blonde wig and transparent dress and to speak with a husky timbre reminiscent of Monroe intensified the parallel to the point of imitation.

After the initial furor died it became apparent to the serious viewer and reader that here was a highly complex work, original in form and serious in theme. Within the year Robert Hogan would predict of *After the Fall* that "its excellence may not clearly emerge until the false glamour of its autobiographical elements has dimmed with time."[3] Onstage throughout the action its hero ponders a problem confronted in other Miller plays: how to make of the outside world a home, a world after the fall from innocence, a world invaded by evil most manifest in the Holocaust but evident as well in personal betrayals. As the play's probing approach requires an equally serious response, it is little wonder that opening-night reviewers slighted the theme and pounced upon the characterization of Maggie. As Miller notes, they treated the play "with barely a mention of any theme, dramatic intention, or style, as though it were simply an attack on a dead woman. . . . It was as though the critics had witnessed an actual domestic quarrel and been challenged to come to Maggie's rescue."[4]

Miller describes the play as a trial by a man's "own conscience, his own values, his own deeds."[5] Appropriately, Quentin is a lawyer. As both prosecutor and defense attorney, he sifts and weighs evidence from the past before he can proceed to a decision about the future. Miller's technique is expressionistic; episodes follow one another not chronologically but, instead, by association, one thought literally leading to another: "The action takes place in the mind, thought, and memory of Quentin." What drives the action is the quest, the search of the hero. Like a Spenserian knight, Quentin seeks a virtue—self-knowledge—with the help of a guide, Holga, who possesses that virtue. Along the way, he will meet and overcome temptations that are sexual (Elsie), moral (deserting his friend Lou), and material (saving his job at Lou's expense). Because Quentin is intellectually honest, he will recognize betrayals, those he commits and those committed against him by his family and by friend Mickey. He will suffer guilt at the horrors of the Holocaust and search for an explanation of its evils. In his experiences with Maggie he will learn that innocence may mask self-serving, and love hatred, and that, when the burden of an unbearably dependent life is lifted, to feel relief is human, though abhorrent. He will see that in the real world, after the Fall, evil cannot be dealt with by denial or even by guilt, but, rather, one must assume responsibility; only then can one hope, love, and forgive.

There are three levels to the nonrealistic setting, a landscape of the mind: a "lava-like, supple geography," with "pits and hollows," where scenes start, and "abutments, ledges, or crevices," where characters rest when inactive. They "appear and disappear instantaneously, as in the mind" for an effect of "the surging, flitting, instantaneousness of a mind questing over its own surfaces and into its depths." The action, therefore, resembles a stream of consciousness in Quentin's mind, making free associations between characters, events, bits of dialogue or gestures, actions, locales, or fleeting images. The one realistic piece of scenery which dominates the stage is "the blasted stone tower of a German concentration camp. Its wide lookout windows are like eyes which at the moment seem blind and dark; bent reinforcing rods stick out of it like broken tentacles." As Quentin recalls people and incidents, they will be picked out by light or disappear into darkness; scenes and dialogue may occur concurrently as well as sequentially, or they may overlap. As with the mind itself, all of the characters are present in the background, from which they may emerge at any time; they appear as a group interacting with Quentin at the beginning and ending of the play.

At the opening of the play Quentin, who is in his forties, separates from the others, advances to the front of the stage (an open stage in the initial production), and addresses an unseen "Listener," who "would be sitting just beyond the edge of the stage itself." The Listener has been variously interpreted as a psychiatrist, priest, judge, God, or the audience itself. Miller says that "The 'Listener,' who to some will be a psychoanalyst, to others God, is Quentin himself turned at the edge of the abyss to look at his experience, his nature and his time."[6] During the action Quentin may be speaking directly to the Listener or participating in one of the episodes or commenting on and interpreting ongoing action. Making the hero a lawyer imposes a certain order on his account, a trial of himself by Quentin, who says, "I looked at life like a case at law."

Quentin examines his two previous marriages for evidence of his responsibility for their failure; he must review these because he has formed a third relationship, with Holga, an Austrian woman who survived World War II and knew its horrors at first hand. Has he the right, he asks the Listener, to become involved with her? Quentin's professional life must be reviewed as well. Just as he suffers guilt for failing his first wife, Louise, and his second, Maggie, so he is plagued by remorse at his relief when friend Lou's suicide saves Quentin from defending him before the House Un-American Activities Committee, a defense that would have cost him his job. Survival, he learns, is a powerful motivation. Family scenes from Quentin's childhood and youth establish a pattern of betrayals. "The underlying principle of taking up a commitment and betraying it, if not the same, is pretty close," observes Miller.[7]

Quentin's personal and professional pressures reflect the larger problem that Quentin explores and attempts to resolve— the existence of evil (symbolized by the concentration camp tower) and the denial of individual responsibility. Miller writes of the inception of *After the Fall:*

I began to search for a form that would unearth the dynamics of denial itself, which seemed to me the massive lie of our time. . . . I saw American culture, the most unfettered on earth, as the culture of denial; even as the drug, in expanding the mind, denied that it was destroying the mind, and the new freedom of sexuality denied that it was dissolving the compassionate self-restraint that made any human relationship conceivable over time. . . . Inevitably the form of the new play was that of a confession, since the main character's quest for a connection to his own life was the issue, his conquest of denial the path into himself.[8]

An event in Quentin's childhood surfaces as Quentin laments to the Listener: "I no longer see some final saving grace! Socialism once, then love; some final hope is gone that always saved before the end!" Learning that everything has been lost in the crash of 1929, his wealthy father is castigated by the mother: "Are you some kind of a moron? . . . Your last dollar! You are an idiot!" "Invisible" young Quentin overhears and begins to cry. His mother denies she has said anything hurtful: "What *I* said? Why, what did I say? . . . Well, I was a little angry, that's all, but I never said *that*. I think he's a wonderful man! [*Laughs.*] How could I say a thing like that?"

Quentin's first wife, Louise, echoes his mother when she says of Quentin, who yearns for connections while she insists on separation: "Good God! What an idiot!" In their final argument Maggie, too, is charged with calling him "idiot in public." The accusations connote contempt for lacking reason, yet an idiot child is a central and positive symbol in the play. It is first mentioned by Holga early in the action, just after Quentin's mother has called his father an idiot. Holga takes up the image in relating a dream that returned, she says, "each night until I dared not go to sleep and grew quite ill": "I dreamed I had a child, and even in the dream I saw it was my life, and it was an idiot, and I ran away. But it always crept onto my lap again, clutched at my clothes. Until I thought, if I could kiss it, whatever in it was my own, perhaps I could sleep. And I bent to its broken face, and it was horrible . . . but I kissed it. I think one must finally take one's life in one's arms, Quentin." It is a lesson Quentin does not learn until the end of the play.

Quentin's two marriages as he reviews them, to Louise mainly in the first act and to Maggie in the second (although episodes echo and overlap one another), reveal that he has searched in vain for a connection within those most permanent-seeming of all unions, marriage and friendship. "It's like some unseen web of connection between people is simply not there," he muses. "And I always relied on it, somehow; I never quite believed that people could be so easily disposed of." Informed that the head of Quentin's firm is urging him to drop the case of friend Lou, Louise recognizes that "Max is not going to endanger his whole firm to defend a Communist. You tend to make relatives out of people."

Although Quentin has not had an extramarital affair, he has been tempted to do so, which Louise regards as betrayal, causing him to feel he is "forever on trial": "Maybe I invite your suspicion in order to—to come down off some bench, to stop judging others so perfectly. Because I do judge, and harshly too, when the fact is I'm bewildered." The first act ends with divorce imminent, when Quentin, hopeful, returns home to report his wonderment at Maggie's innocence: "I felt strangely abstract beside her. And I saw that we are killing one another with abstractions." Louise misinterprets the incident: "You don't want me." "To himself," Quentin comments: "God! Can that be true?"

Depicted through Quentin's eyes, Louise is portrayed as cold and self-centered. Although they may have been in love when they married, what Quentin now recalls is the death of love, superseded by suspicion, accusation, betrayal, and guilt. Louise reappears from time to time insisting, "I'm not all this uninteresting"; the truth is that she is uninteresting. Miller keeps the Louise incidents brief, interspersing Quentin's childhood memories and professional associations with friends Lou and Mickey. Summoned before the congressional investigating committee, wealthy

Mickey will "name names" of long-ago socialist sympathizers—including Lou and Quentin—in order to "clear" himself in the interest of "truth." Lou charges him with betrayal: "It astounds me that you can speak of truth and justice in relation to that gang of cheap publicity hounds!" He concludes: "There is only one truth here. You are terrified! They have bought your soul!"

The figures of Felice, a dancer, and Elsie, Lou's wife, flit in and out of Quentin's thoughts. Felice, whose divorce case Quentin has handled successfully, idolizes him and insists on "blessing" him, although this makes him uncomfortable: "I think it had to do with power. . . . I wish to God—*Felice raises her arm*—she'd stop blessing me! . . . Well, I suppose because there is a fraud involved; I have no such power." Felice is associated with Quentin's mother, who also idolized him and of whose blessing he was always aware. She felt that the child was destined for greatness and enlisted him as an "accomplice" against his father. In Quentin's early sequences with Maggie, Felice appears fleetingly, as Quentin remarks to the Listener, "I do, yes, I see the similarity." Both Felice and Maggie attribute to Quentin a power that changed their lives.

Unlike Maggie and Felice, who are sympathetically portrayed, Elsie is a tempter. She appears naked and inviting before Quentin (who declines the invitation), betraying her husband, Lou, Quentin's friend and client. Serpentlike, she tempts Louise with knowledge; through the psychoanalysis Elsie encourages, Louise's resentments against Quentin surface, find a voice, and lead to their divorce.

Appearing and reappearing throughout the play is Holga, an Austrian whom Quentin has befriended in Germany. A symbol rather than a full-blown character like Maggie or even Louise, Holga carries the burden of the theme. She already has attained the self-knowledge Quentin seeks. "Holga teaches him the necessary lesson that guilt, loss, and betrayal are not punishments to be avoided but inevitable signs of the human condition."[9] Her remarks about the idiot child are not understood by Quentin until late in the action. When they visit the concentration camp, whose monster-like tower looms above the setting, it is she who assuages Quentin's feelings of guilt about the Holocaust by assuring him that "no one they didn't kill can be innocent again." Miller indicates that "the basic thrust of the play is that the enemy is innocence. . . . until you can give up your innocence, you are very open to crime, to becoming part of the crime."[10]

The Maggie episodes, as they develop emotionally rather than chronologically, provide the dramatic impact necessary to balance the play's intellectual appeal. Quentin's disastrous romance with and marriage to Maggie, followed by her suicide attempts, occupy the greater part of act 2. Painful as it obviously was for Miller to create a stage figure resembling Marilyn Monroe, Maggie emerges as a convincing character in her own right, presented with insight and understanding. The Maggie plot is integral to the intellectual thrust of the work, echoing its theme in terms of human relationship and commitment. Twenty-three years later Miller would write in his autobiography of the heartbreaking agony of this marriage. In an article in *Life* magazine shortly after the opening, however, Miller insists on a broader view for the play: "the character of Maggie . . . is not in fact Marilyn Monroe. Maggie is a character in a play about the human animal's unwillingness or inability to discover in himself the seeds of his own destruction.... She most perfectly exemplifies the self-destructiveness which finally comes when one views oneself as pure victim. And she . . . exemplifies this view because she comes so close to being a pure victim—of parents, of a Puritanical sexual code and of her exploitation as an entertainer."[11]

Miller first thought of a character like Maggie in the 1950s in a play he later abandoned, about research physicians: "Into their midst comes the mistress of Dr. Tibbets, Lorraine, a character modeled rather distantly on Marilyn, whom I still barely knew. With her open sexuality, childlike and sublimely free of ties and expectations in a life she half senses is doomed," she brings tragedy to the men. "Like a blind, godlike force, with all its creative cruelty, her sexuality comes to seem the only truthful connection with some ultimate nature, everything that is life-giving and authentic. . . . but she has no security of her own and no faith, and her liberating promise is finally illusory."[12]

Almost four years after Quentin's first encounter with Maggie, then a receptionist, she has become a famous singer. She attributes her changed life to him: "I would do anything for you Quentin—you're like a god!" Quentin addresses the Listener: "The first honor was that I hadn't tried to go to bed with her! She took it for a tribute to her 'value,' and I was only afraid! God, the hypocrisy!"

Maggie fears and is haunted by her mother, who, like Monroe's, was promiscuous in her behavior and puritanical in her outlook. Quentin's own mother appears, in an incident of early betrayal. She is knocking at a locked door, holding a toy boat souvenir, and insisting, "But darling, we didn't trick you." Quentin explains to the Listener: "They sent me out for a walk with the maid. When I came back the house was empty. God, why is betrayal the only truth that sticks? I adored that woman."

In *Timebends* Miller also associates Monroe with his mother:

> Even after only those few hours with Marilyn, she had taken on an immanence in my imagination, the vitality of a force one does not understand but that seems on the verge of lighting up a vast surrounding plain of darkness. I was struggling to . . . understand why I felt as though I had lost a sort of sanction that I had seemed to possess since earliest childhood. . . . I needed the benediction of something or someone. . . . Someone, I had always supposed, was secretly watching over me unseen. It was of course the mother, the first audience—actually the concept of her in a most primordial sense that perhaps only the boy-child, half lover and half rebel against her dominion, really knows in his mythifying blood.[13]

The appearances of the mother throughout the play, notes Iska Alter, recapitulate "maternal seduction, betrayal, or abandonment," as a "reminder of the ongoing authority of the female imperium."[14] Near the end of the play Maggie and the mother will be linked in a strong visual image of attempted destruction.

Maggie assures Quentin: "I . . . don't really sleep around with everybody. I was with a lot of men but I never got anything for it. It was like charity, see? My analyst said I gave to those in need." When she reports that her agent advised her to make him her beneficiary, Quentin explodes: "It's not the money they take, it's the dignity that they destroy." He insists, "You're serious, you're first-class, people *mean* something to you; you don't have to go begging shady people for advice like some—some tramp!" "[*He . . . suddenly lifts her, and with immense pity and hope:*] Maggie, stand up!"

At the same time, because he is honest, Quentin must admit to the Listener: "How can you speak of love, she was chewed and spat out by a long line of grinning men! Her name floating in the stench of locker rooms and parlor car cigar smoke! She had the truth that day, I brought the lie that she had to be 'saved'! From what? Except my own contempt!"

After they marry Maggie's jealousy, temperamental outbursts, extravagances, vulgar language, and accusations are all attempts to antagonize him so that she can once again see herself as a victim. In a last scene together she even tries to make him take the bottle of sleeping pills, so that she can wrest it from him, thus making him, Quentin realizes, her killer: "You take your death from me. Something in you has been setting me up for a murder." He's leaving her, he says, "so you're not my victim any more." She already has attempted suicide twice, and twice he has saved her: "A suicide kills two people, Maggie, that's what it's for! So I'm removing myself, and perhaps it will lose its point."

When Maggie asks what has happened to their relationship, he replies: "Maggie, we . . . used one another!" Maggie clings to denial: "Not me, not me!" But Quentin insists:

You eat those pills to blind yourself, but if you could only say, "I have been cruel," this frightening room would open. If you could say, "I have been kicked around, but I have been just as inexcusably vicious to others, called my

husband idiot in public, I have been utterly selfish despite
my generosity, I have been hurt by a long line of men but I
have cooperated with my persecutors—"

MAGGIE: . . . Son of a bitch!

QUENTIN: "And I am full of hatred; I, Maggie, sweet
lover of all life—I hate the world!"

MAGGIE: Get out of here!

QUENTIN: "Hate women, hate men, hate all who will not
grovel at my feet proclaiming my limitless love for ever
and ever!" But no pill can make us innocent. Throw them in
the sea, throw death in the sea and all your innocence. Do
the hardest thing of all—see your own hatred and live!

She swallows a handful of pills; he grabs her wrist and then
"lunges for her throat" but springs away as he hears his mother's
voice shouting through the door, repeating the earlier episode, "I
didn't trick you!" His mother "backs into his hand, which of its
own volition, begins to squeeze her throat," in one of Miller's
most startling images. Quentin recounts to the Listener that
Maggie survives this encounter but dies a few months later:
"Barbiturates kill by suffocation. And the signal is a kind of
sighing." He hears "those deep, unnatural breaths, like the
footfalls of my coming peace—and knew . . . I wanted them. How
is that possible? I loved that girl!"

The play reaches its conclusion as Quentin, approaching the
tower, realizes: "Who can be innocent again on this mountain of
skulls? I tell you what I know! My brothers died here. . . . but my
brothers built this place. . . . And what's the cure? . . . No, not love;
I loved them all, all! And gave them willing to failure and to death

that I might live, as they gave me and gave each other, with a word, a look, a trick, a truth, a lie—and all in love!" Holga appears, with her greeting, the word that opens and closes the play, "Hello!" Quentin cries, "That woman hopes!" and realizes that "she hopes, because she knows." As Miller explains, "no man knows himself who cannot face the murder in him, the sly and everlasting complicity with the forces of destruction."[15]

Quentin's final realization, and the conclusion of his trial by his own mind and conscience, paradoxically both finds him guilty and sets him free to hope, for Holga is the embodiment of hope; she can hope because she knows "what burning cities taught her and the death of love taught me: that we are very dangerous!"

Miller describes his style in *After the Fall* as "impressionistic": "I was trying to create a total by throwing many small pieces at the spectator." He believes that Zeffirelli's Italian production of the play best recognized that "the mounting awareness of this man was the issue, and as it approached agony the audience was to be enlarged in its consciousness of what was happening." Other productions, he notes, have been "*realistic* in the worst sense. . . . they simply played the scenes without any attempt to allow the main character to develop this widened awareness. He has different reactions on page ten than he does on page one, but it takes an actor with a certain amount of brains to see that evolution."[16] Miller may be implying his disappointment with the original presentation of the play, directed by Elia Kazan, with Jason Robards as Quentin, in a production that was long on realism "in the worst sense" and short on creating an impressionistic effect.[17]

AFTER THE FALL **AND** *INCIDENT AT VICHY*

After the Fall is poetic both in its dramatic effects and in its language. Miller uses dramatically the free associations that modern poetry uses verbally. All of the women are subtly connected in Quentin's mind—Louise's complaint that she is "not all that uninteresting" is echoed in a positive way by Holga's awareness that she "may not be all that interesting" to Quentin, whose mind is probing the Jungian riddle of complicity.[18] The hope Holga symbolizes in her intermittent appearances reflects the hope Quentin inexplicably feels each morning, a refrain that occurs at the beginning of the play, at the end of act 1, and at the end of the play: "I wake each morning like a boy—even now, even now! I swear to you, I could love the world again!"

The play abounds in symbolism. *The Magic Flute,* which Holga recommends, aptly symbolizes a trial by fire which love must survive; Lazarus, about whom Maggie asks Quentin, suggests resurrection and hope, life from death. The tower, observes Stephen S. Stanton, is a symbol of the "extension of guilt from the personal to the social" level.[19] The interrelationship of betrayals on the personal, professional, and social levels finds effective expression in Miller's impressionistic style. The mother's deception of the child Quentin is linked to Maggie's showing Quentin the deceptive will her agent has drawn in his favor. In their first sexual encounter, "the lie that she had to be 'saved'" evokes Quentin's recollection of defending Reverend Barnes and at the same time attacking him.

Quentin's "mounting awareness" approaching "agony" is expressed in increasingly poetic dialogue. In the second act, as Maggie's speech changes from childlike questions that invoke protection to bitter and cynical invective, Quentin's dialogue grows more varied in length and structure, more lyric in diction. His final realization is very possibly Miller's best poetry in all his plays, for its rhythm, imagery, simplicity, and perfect match of theme and expression:

> Is the knowing all? To know, and even happily, that we meet unblessed; not in some garden of wax fruit and painted trees, that lie of Eden, but after, after the Fall, after many, many deaths. Is the knowing all? And the wish to kill is never killed, but with some gift of courage one may look into its face when it appears, and with a stroke of love—as to an idiot in the house—forgive it; again and again . . . forever?

Incident at Vichy

The central idea of *Incident at Vichy,* says Miller, continues the theme of *After the Fall*—"that when we live in a time of great murders, we are inhabiting a world of murder for which we share the guilt. . . . We have an investment in evils that we manage to escape, that sometimes those evils that we oppose are done in our interest. . . . By virtue of these circumstances, a man is faced with his own complicity with what he despises."[20]

The play was requested by producers Robert Whitehead and Harold Clurman to follow *After the Fall* at the temporary theater, as Lincoln Center was still under construction. Knowing he could draw on "a superior acting company," says Miller, he began and completed *Incident at Vichy* "in a short time." Had he "been fortunate enough to live in a period when a high-level repertory or art theater existed," he reflects, he would have written more plays.

A psychoanalyst "who had hidden out in Vichy France during the war, before the Nazis openly occupied the country," told Miller a story that suggested the plot: "a Jewish analyst picked up with false papers and saved by a man he had never seen before. This unknown man, a gentile, had substituted himself in a line of suspects waiting to have their papers and penises inspected in a hunt for Jews posing as Frenchmen."[21] "What *Incident at Vichy* reiterates is our proclivity to evade troublesome facts so that confrontation with evil and hence our responsibility for it are avoided."[22]

In Vichy in the waiting room of "a place of detention" in 1942 ten men seated in a row await questioning by the authorities. In charge is a young Nazi major on injury leave from battle; the other authorities are French. The suspects are summoned one by one into an unseen inner room, where the Police Captain reigns, assisted by two detectives and a "professor" of "racial anthropology." Some of the suspects will be released and depart, pass in hand, through the waiting area past the single guard. Others will not be seen again. The hopes and fears of the detainees are revealed, and dramatic tension builds as each is called in, until only the doctor and the prince are left. The occupation, appearance, behavior, and outlook of each of the suspects individualizes him and engages the sympathy as well as the suspense of the audience, even though Miller notes that he was "not attempting to delineate psychological types. . . . The characters were functions of the society."[23]

UNDERSTANDING ARTHUR MILLER

Although the men are all "anxious and frightened," at first they try to overcome their fears with assurances that the questioning is only routine; as long as their papers are in order, they will be discharged or, at worst, put to work as "volunteer" laborers. A waiter among them even assures them that the Nazi major, a customer at his restaurant, is "not a really bad fellow." When the Police Captain takes one of the detectives aside to instruct him, the audience learns how the men are being taken off the streets: "Just cruise around the way we did before, and take them one at a time. There are all kinds of rumors. We don't want to alarm people."

Soon evidence begins to emerge that only Jews are being picked up. Bayard, an electrician for the railway, discloses that a train has arrived from Toulouse with locked cars from which cries were heard; that the engineer is Polish suggests Auschwitz. Monceau, a complacent, self-assured actor, claims that even at Auschwitz Jews have nothing to fear—his cousin there is being taught bricklaying. "The important thing," he says, "is not to look like a victim. Or even to feel like one," for "they do have a sense for victims." He concludes: "You are trying to create an illusion; to make them believe you are who your papers say you are." Leduc, the psychiatrist, observes, "That's true; we must not play the part they have written for us."

When Marchand, a confident businessman, is questioned and released with a pass, the other suspects take heart. Then the waiter's boss, bringing coffee for the authorities, whispers briefly to his employee before departing in tears. In shock the waiter passes the news to the other men: "He heard the detectives; they came in for coffee just before. People get burned up in furnaces.

It's not to work. They burn you up in Poland." Monceau, the disbeliever, is unaware of the dramatic irony of his response: "That is the most fantastic idiocy I ever heard in my life!"

Von Berg, a Catholic Austrian prince, has been arrested by mistake; he believes the detectives heard his foreign accent. When Bayard asserts a communistic belief in the future, "when the working class is master of the world," Von Berg points out that "ninety-nine percent of the Nazis are ordinary working-class people! . . . They adore Hitler."

Noticing that there is only one guard at the door, Leduc suggests that they overpower him and escape. No one volunteers to assist him. Leduc tries to enlist actor Monceau, who replies, "I refuse to play a part I do not fit." The departing boss of the waiter reminds him that he was warned "fifty times to get out of this city!" Lebeau confides that he and his parents could have emigrated to America before the German invasion; but his mother wouldn't go: "She had this brass bed, and carpets, and draperies and all kinds of junk" which she refused to leave. "People won't believe they can be killed. Not them with their brass bed and their carpets and their faces."

A Gypsy evokes varied responses, including the same prejudices as held against the Jews. Bayard worries that the Gypsy's detention signals a roundup of those categorized as "inferior" under the "Racial Laws." Some suspect that the pot the Gypsy carries may have been stolen, though Lebeau tells him, "All property is theft anyway so I've got no prejudice against you." Completing the group of detainees are an Old Jew, bearded and carrying a large bundle, who silently rocks back and forth in prayer, and a young boy of fifteen. The boy had ventured out to pawn his mother's wedding ring to buy food for their starving family, and, as hope fades, he begs Von Berg, certain to be released, to take the ring and return it.

Aristocrat Von Berg and psychiatrist Leduc, the final two remaining, demonstrate in word and action the theme of the play. Von Berg says: "I would like to be able to part with your friendship. Is that possible?" Leduc replies that he is not angry with him: "I am only angry that I should have been born before the day when man has accepted his own nature; that he is *not* reasonable, that he is full of murder, that his ideas are only the little tax he pays for the right to hate and kill with a clear conscience." When he states that he believes gentiles have "a dislike if not a hatred for the Jews," Von Berg denies that this is true of him. Leduc replies:

> Until you know it is true of you, you will destroy whatever truth can come of this atrocity. Part of knowing who we are is knowing we are not someone else. And Jew is only the name we give to that stranger, that agony we cannot feel, that death we look at like a cold abstraction. Each man has his Jew; it is the other. And the Jews have their Jews. And now, now above all, you must see that you have yours—the man whose death leaves you relieved that you are not him, despite your decency. And that is why there is nothing and will be nothing—until you face your own complicity with this . . . your own humanity.

Von Berg again denies any relationship to "this monstrousness," for he even tried to kill himself when the Nazis murdered his Jewish musicians. Leduc discloses that Von Berg's beloved cousin is a Nazi who persecuted Jewish doctors: "If you had understood that Baron Kessler was in part, in some part, in some small and frightful part—doing your will. You might have done something then, with your standing, and your name and your decency, aside from shooting yourself!" Leduc drives home his point: "It's not your guilt I want, it's your responsibility." Von Berg cries out, "What can ever save us?" The door opens, and the prince is summoned to the inner room.

He emerges a few moments later with a pass. He thrusts it with the wedding ring into Leduc's hand: "Take it! Go!" Leduc, "in the awareness of his own guilt," pleads: "I wasn't asking you to do this! You don't owe me this!" Von Berg insists, "Go!" As the guard appears at the end of the corridor, Leduc hands him the pass and disappears. The Professor enters to call in the next suspect, sees Von Berg, shouts an alarm, and sirens sound; the Major rushes in and "with a look of anguish and fury," his fists clenched, confronts Von Berg. The two stand there, "forever incomprehensible to one another, looking into each other's eyes." Four new prisoners are ushered in to sit on the bench, looking about at their surroundings and "the two men staring at each other so strangely," as the play ends.

Although the reviews were generally favorable, some of them charged the characters with being "symbols," to which Edward Murray replies, noting that Leduc, Von Berg, and the Major "grow" in the course of the action.[24] Both Leduc and Von Berg, through argument and counterargument, are able to learn and to change previously held viewpoints.

The Major is one of the earliest sympathetic portrayals of a Nazi by an American. Wounded in battle, he has been assigned against his will to head the investigation. When he is prevented by the Professor from leaving for a brief respite, he then escapes in alcohol and, "'high' with drink," tells Leduc, "I would only like to say that . . . this is all as inconceivable to me as it is to you." Leduc replies: "I'd believe it if you shot yourself. And better yet, if you took a few of them with you." But the youthful, despairing Major points out they would all be replaced: "There are no persons any more." Shooting off his pistol into the ceiling, he challenges Leduc to tell him "how there can be persons any more. I have you at the end of this revolver—[*indicates the Professor*] he has me—and somebody has him—and somebody has somebody else."

Educated, well dressed and well spoken, Von Berg knows little about the reality of the war or the desperation of the times. A patron of music, he has withdrawn into his comfortable villa, and it is only when the Nazis affect him personally by shooting his musicians that he thinks of killing himself. And yet, he tells Leduc: "when I told the story to many of my friends there was hardly any reaction. That was almost worse." Von Berg learns the most, for Leduc's realization is a conclusion to which his earlier arguments have been leading. But it is Von Berg who demonstrates, by giving up his pass and probably his life, that it is not enough to assume guilt; one must also assume responsibility.

As Leduc's speeches drive home the theme expressed in the action, Miller again demonstrates his unique ability to dramatize ideas. From the beginning Leduc is the most rational, as he questions the arrest. Urging the others to join him in subduing the single guard, and having been told the situation cannot be serious if there is only one guard, Leduc fathoms that the enemy is relying on them "to project our own reasonable ideas into their heads. It is reasonable that a light guard means the thing is not important. They rely on our own logic to immobilize ourselves." Each of the others interprets the situation personally; only Leduc sees the universal. Leduc's final speeches cause Von Berg to act and the play to achieve its intellectual and emotional climax.

Tension mounts as each man is summoned to the inner room where his life or death will be decided. As symbols, the inner room represents the unknown future or death itself, while the detention area is a limbo where judgment is awaited. The irony is that the Police Captain, the detectives, and the "Professor" are so ill qualified to judge; the waiting area is an anteroom of Hell. Reminders of the outside world and of the comforts of a home, now far removed, intrude constantly: the wedding ring, Leduc's wife and children, Lebeau's parents and their possessions. Perhaps the most evocative symbol of home, in contrast to the cold, impersonal detention room, is the bundle the Old Jew clutches. When he is forced from his seat, his bundle is torn from him. Surprisingly, "a white cloud of feathers blows up"; they swirl about and float down, reminders of pillows and beds and home.

Although the play is set in World War II, it has remained timely since its premiere in 1964. "The occasion of the play is the occupation of France, but it's about today," Miller told Barbara Gelb. "It concerns the question of insight—of seeing in oneself the capacity for collaboration with the evil one condemns. It's a question that exists for all of us." Each "pursuit and profession," he noted, is "dominated by its own logic, totally unconcerned with any overall judgment of values, any sense of complicity or willingness to assume responsibility."[25]

Notes

1. Robert Brustein, "Arthur Miller's *Mea Culpa,*" *New Republic*, 8 February 1964, 26–27.

2. Leslie Hanscom, "*After the Fall:* Arthur Miller's Return," *Newsweek*, 3 February 1964, 50–51.

3. Robert Hogan, *Arthur Miller* (Minneapolis: University of Minnesota Press, 1964), 40.

4. Arthur Miller, *Timebends* (New York: Grove Press, 1987), 534.

5. Arthur Miller, "A Foreword by the Author," *After the Fall, Saturday Evening Post*, 1 February 1964, 32.

6. Ibid.

7. Arthur Miller, "After the Fall," in *Arthur Miller and Company,* ed. Christopher Bigsby (London: Methuen Drama, 1990), 139.

8. Miller, *Timebends,* 520–21.

9. Iska Alter, "Betrayal and Blessedness: Explorations of Feminine Power in *The Crucible, A View from the Bridge,* and *After the Fall,*" in *Feminist Rereadings of Modern American Drama,* ed. June Schlueter (Rutherford, N.J.: Fairleigh Dickinson University Press, 1989), 142.

10. Miller, *Arthur Miller and Company,* 139.

11. Arthur Miller, "With Respect for Her Agony—but with Love," *Life*, 7 February 1964, 66.

12. Miller, *Timebends,* 326.

13. Ibid., 327.

14. Alter, "Betrayal and Blessedness," 137.

15. Miller, "A Foreword," *Saturday Evening Post,* 32.

16. Olga Carlisle and Rose Styron, "Arthur Miller: An Interview," in *The Theater Essays of Arthur Miller,* ed. Robert A. Martin (New York: Viking Press, 1978), 282–83.

17. Elia Kazan describes the production in *A Life* (New York: Knopf, 1988), 666–69.

18. C. G. Jung, *The Undiscovered Self* (London: Routledge and Kegan Paul, 1958), 95–96.

19. Stephen S. Stanton, "Pessimism in *After the Fall,"* in *Arthur Miller: New Perspectives,* ed. Robert A. Martin (Englewood Cliffs, N.J.: Prentice-Hall, 1982), 171.

20. Richard I. Evans, *Psychology and Arthur Miller* (New York: Praeger, 1981), 74.

21. Miller, *Timebends,* 538.

22. Harold Clurman, "Editor's Introduction," *The Portable Arthur Miller* (New York: Viking Press, 1971), xix.

23. Josh Greenfeld, "'Writing Plays Is Absolutely Senseless,' Arthur Miller Says, 'But I Love It. I Just Love It,'" *New York Times Magazine,* 13 February 1972, 37.

24. Edward Murray, *Arthur Miller, Dramatist* (New York: Ungar, 1967), 170.

25. Barbara Gelb, "Question: 'Am I My Brother's Keeper?'" *New York Times,* 29 November 1964, sec. 2, p. 1.

CHAPTER EIGHT

The Price

The conflict between father and sons, a recurrent Miller theme, is seen in *The Price* from the viewpoint of the sons. Although absent from the action, father Franz has determined the characters and the destinies of his sons, Walter and Victor. In a room crowded with the furniture of their youth the brothers meet after sixteen years of estrangement to reexamine old values and to learn that a price must be paid in the present for choices made in the past. As they alternately defend and accuse, almost as if on trial, the unlikely arbiter is an eighty-nine-year-old secondhand dealer appropriately named Solomon. A surrogate father, he sits in the paternal chair, commenting, sympathizing, reprimanding, and advising before counting out the money that symbolizes the prices paid for the decisions of a lifetime.

The action is deceptively simple. As the house of his dead parents is about to be demolished, policeman Victor meets Solomon to negotiate a price for the furniture. Victor has left a message at the office of his brother, now a successful surgeon, to attend and approve the sale. In their two-hour encounter each reevaluates earlier family crises, blames the other and defends himself, and recognizes, if not fully accepting, responsibility for past actions and present outcomes. Although the dialogue seems convincingly realistic and the time of the action is actual and continuous, Miller's visual and verbal symbolism, his characterization of the contrasting brothers in a common family situation, and his creation of the all-wise though comic Solomon demonstrate the universality of *The Price*.

THE PRICE

That Miller views conflict between brothers as mythic can be seen in his choice of Cain and Abel as antagonists in his next play, *The Creation of the World and Other Business* (1972). Victor's and Walter's initial disagreement centers upon an acceptable price for the piled-up items; deeper resentments surface as they relive the past which is conjured up by the furniture. Idealistic younger brother Victor sacrificed his college degree and the hope of a professional career to support his father, psychologically immobilized when his prosperous business was wiped out by the market crash of 1929. Struck by the failure of his father, Victor chose the noncompetitive job of a civil servant; now, nearing the age of fifty, he is undecided about retiring from the police force.

In act 1, before Walter arrives, there is tension but also affection between Victor and his wife, Esther. She complains that he is owed a "moral debt" for shouldering the burden of their father, allowing Walter to attend medical school and attain wealth and fame. Assuming that the money paid for the furniture should go to Victor, she is there to see that he gets a good price: "We can never keep our minds on money! We worry about it, we talk about it, but we can't seem to *want* it. I do, but you don't. I really do, Vic. I want it. Vic? *I want money!*" Her outburst is understandable, for all their married life they have scraped along on his modest salary. To her the money to be paid for the furniture represents all the small comforts they could never afford. In act 2, when Walter offers Victor a considerable amount (if the furniture becomes a tax-deductible donation), Esther is even more insistent that Victor be rewarded materially for his earlier sacrifices. Ashamed to be seen in public with him in uniform, she leaves to collect his civilian jacket.

Alone with Solomon, Victor agrees that it is "impossible to

know what is important," and recalls his disappointments in life: making decisions when unaware of the outcome, like dropping out of school to support his father. "We always agreed, we stay out of the rat race and live our own life. That was important. But you shovel the crap out the window, it comes back under the door—it all ends up she wants, she wants. And I can't really blame her—there's just no respect for anything but money." At the very end of the first act, just as Victor has accepted the price and is receiving Solomon's money, Walter appears. He is equally unhappy. Successful, in his mid-fifties, he seldom sees the children of his broken marriage, and he has suffered a nervous breakdown. He bears the added burden of guilt for deserting his father to pursue a career. In the course of the afternoon, with unsought advice from Solomon, Walter will attempt to justify his actions by arguing that Victor also should have thought of himself and attended college; their seemingly helpless and destitute father actually had thousands.

Amid the recriminations and accusations of act 2, Victor portrays himself as the loyal son and Walter as selfish for refusing his brother's request for a college tuition loan. Walter, however, sees Victor as a dupe and regards himself as a realist, unblinded by the myth of family ties: "There was nothing here but a straight financial arrangement. . . . And you proceeded to wipe out what you saw."

In his "Author's Production Note" at the end of the published text Miller cautions the actors of Victor and Walter to maintain "a fine balance of sympathy." Walter, notes Miller, "is attempting to put into action what he has learned about himself," and the actor "must not regard his attempts to win back Victor's friendship as mere manipulation." The author explains "the theme of the play": "As the world now operates, the qualities of both brothers are necessary to it; surely their respective psychologies and moral values conflict at the heart of the social dilemma." He states that "the production must therefore withhold judgment in favor of presenting both men in all their humanity and from their own viewpoints. Actually, each has merely proved to the other what the other has known but dared not face. At the end, demanding of one another what was forfeited to time, each is left touching the structure of his life."

Miller's insistence that the production be fair and balanced in evoking sympathy for both brothers did not earn him critical approval. Not one to cater to the expectations of the audience or the critics, Miller explained in an NBC television interview in August 1968 that in *The Price:* "I've done something which is probably intolerable, I've suspended judgment. I've simply shown you what happens when you take these two courses and the price you pay for being responsible, and the price you pay for being irresponsible and hopefully it would agitate people to think about this." In his plays, the author noted, "you are pretty well cued in to what's happening from moment to moment and ultimately you arrive at a paradox which, because I think I don't let you off the hook, is quite intolerable. You want me to tell you what to think."

The paradox at which *The Price* arrives in the second act is as true as it is ingenious. The audience is prepared to see Walter through Victor's eyes until Walter arrives with a different interpretation of past events. As Gerald Weales points out, *The Price* is an extremely talky play, blending "psychoanalysis with Ibsenite revelation."[1] The revelation or "paradox" in act 2 builds dramatic tension and reveals more fully the characters of the brothers. A favorite Miller theme, truth versus illusion, emerges as they reexamine the past and the motives for Victor's remaining with their father and Walter's leaving home.

The setting offers visual proof of the family's lost wealth. Heavy, solid furniture, expensive in its day, is piled up in the attic room to which Victor and his father retreated. Existing on "garbage," throwaway scraps from restaurants, the elder Franz refused to leave the overstuffed armchair (at center stage), where he sat listening to the radio and cared for by Victor, who cooked on a hotplate and slept on a cot.[2]

Victor recalls that Walter, asked for a loan for college tuition, replied, "Ask Dad for money." When Victor does so, the father merely laughs. Trying to understand, Victor walks to a park behind the library. In an emotional outburst he reveals why he could not desert his father, blamed by his mother and abandoned by Walter:

The grass was covered with men. Like a battlefield; a big open-air flophouse. And not bums—some of them still had shined shoes and good hats, busted businessmen, lawyers, skilled mechanics. Which I'd seen a hundred times. But suddenly—you know?—I *saw* it. . . . There was no mercy. Anywhere. . . . One day you're the head of the house , at the head of the table, and suddenly you're shit. Overnight. And I tried to figure out that laugh. How could he be holding out on me when he loved me?

THE PRICE

Walter, however, quickly dispels Victor's contention that they were brought up to believe in each other, that only he could save their father: "Were we really brought up to believe in one another?" he asks. "We were brought up to succeed, weren't we? Why else would he respect me so and not you?" He reminds Victor of their father's laugh when Victor needed him: "What you saw behind the library was not that there was no mercy in the world, kid. It's that there was no love in this house. There was no loyalty. There was nothing here but a straight financial arrangement. That's what was unbearable."

What sustains the dramatic intensity is what makes courtroom drama so fascinating: a convincing defense is immediately countered by an attack similarly convincing. As soon as one brother has justified his behavior, he is undercut by the other's opposing interpretation. David Thacker, who directed the play for a production at the Young Vic in London, reports that Miller stressed "the dialectical nature of the play: every argument posed is matched instantly by a counter-argument and then countered again. Each must be given equal weight and force. He was anxious that the audience should not stand in judgment on Victor or Walter. . . . The play, he said, was finally about love. The brothers love each other and want to come together, but can't."[3]

Walter's insistence that they "were brought up to succeed" would explain his determination to leave the father, attend medical school, and achieve fame as a surgeon. But it also reveals why the crash psychologically paralyzed their father and why Victor chose a job unthreatened by failure. (Despite his own choice, Victor in act 1 brags that his son, away at college, is invincible: "a terrific boy . . . nobody's ever going to take that guy.") After the elder Franz's success ended in disaster, Walter was motivated even more strongly to succeed, but this led to a breakdown. In the "Production Note" Miller states: "From entrance to exit, Walter is attempting to put into action what he has learned about himself, and sympathy will be evoked for him in proportion to the openness, the depth of need, the intimations of suffering with which the role is played."

Walter tries to explain to Victor and Esther how he has changed after starting out "wanting to be the best": "The time comes when you realize that you haven't merely been specializing in something—something has been specializing in you. . . . And the whole thing comes down to fear," he tells them, "the slow, daily fear you call ambition, and cautiousness, and piling up the money." But when he began taking risks, he says, "suddenly I saw something else. And it was terror." When Victor asks, "Terror of what?" Walter responds: "Of it ever happening to me . . . as it happened to him. Overnight, for no reason, to find yourself degraded and thrown down." He asks, "You know what I'm talking about, don't you? [VICTOR *turns away slightly, refusing commitment.*] Isn't that why you turned your back on it all?" Victor replies, "sensing the relevancy to himself now": "Partly. Not altogether, though."

Having had to face some painful truths about his own life, Walter has succeeded in evoking this confession from Victor, even though he only "partly" admits it. There is more to come. Walter is anxious that Victor accept at least some of the responsibility for his sacrifices and that all of the blame not be attributed to Walter's desertion and his refusal to lend Victor money for college. Walter reveals that he telephoned their father to offer to pay the tuition (a message never delivered), insisting that his brother should not join the police force and waste his "fine mind." The father's reply was: "Victor wants to help me. I can't stop him."

Walter's final revelation is even more painful to Victor: all the time Victor had been supporting him, their father had nearly four thousand dollars. He had asked Walter to invest that sum for him, believing that "sooner or later" Victor would desert him. Victor claims he had no choice but to remain. Walter points to the harp: "Even then it was worth a couple of hundred, maybe more! Your degree was right there." That Walter does feel some responsibility for his brother's lost opportunities is evident in his offer of an administrative post in his hospital. Victor's response is an angry one: "Why do you have to offer me anything?" "There's a price people have to pay. I've paid it, it's all gone, I haven't got it any more. Just like you paid, didn't you? You've got no wife, you've lost your family, you're rattling around all over the place?"

After they have relived the past crises, denied personal responsibility, and defended their earlier decisions, there is some hope that the brothers might at last resolve their differences. As Miller notes: "they think they have achieved the indifference to the betrayals of the past that maturity confers. But it all comes back; the old angry symbols evoke the old emotions of injustice, and they part unreconciled. Neither can accept that the world needs both of them—the dutiful man of order and the ambitious, selfish creator who invents new cures."[4]

Although for thirty years he strove to prevent the kind of catastrophe his father suffered, Walter has learned a painful truth: "I only got out alive when I saw that there was no catastrophe, there never had been." He feels that, if Victor could recognize his past self-delusion, they could meet without recrimination:

> We invent ourselves, Vic, to wipe out what we know. You invent a life of self-sacrifice, a life of duty; but what never existed here cannot be upheld. You were not upholding something, you were denying what you knew they [their parents] were. And denying yourself. And that's all that is standing between us now—an illusion, Vic. That I kicked them in the face and you must uphold them against me. But I only saw then what you see now—there was nothing here to betray. I am not your enemy. It is all an illusion and if you could walk through it, we could meet.

But they cannot meet, and their accusations mount to a climax. Victor tries to force Walter to confess "some wish to hold [him] back."

VICTOR: You came for the old handshake, didn't you! The okay! . . . And you end up with the respect, the career, the money, and best of all, the thing that nobody else can tell you so you can believe it—that you're one hell of a guy and never harmed anybody in your life! Well, you won't get it, not till I get mine!

WALTER: And you? You never had any hatred for me? Never a wish to see me destroyed? To destroy me, to destroy me with this saintly self-sacrifice, this mockery of sacrifice?

THE PRICE

Crying "You will never, never again make me ashamed!" and flinging their mother's gown at Victor, Walter leaves. His wild behavior alarms Victor: "Maybe he oughtn't go into the street like that—." But Solomon advises him: "Let him go. . . . What can you do?" In the place of the father, in whose chair he has been sitting, Solomon offers Victor the wisest course of action.

Described by Miller as "a phenomenon," Solomon is an original, both wise and antic: Miller's creation, for modern times, of an Elizabethan wise fool, with a Russian Yiddish accent. Solomon personifies the theme of the play: on the realistic level he examines, evaluates, and offers a price for the actual furniture of the Franz household; in a symbolic parallel Victor and Walter reassess bygone days which the furniture evokes, reevaluate choices made then, and realize the price each has paid for past actions. Victor is unable to trust Walter in the present because of his behavior twenty-eight years ago. But, as Solomon observes when Victor insists it is good furniture, "I was also very good; now I'm not so good. Time, you know, is a terrible thing." With comments applied to the furniture but analogous to the brothers' relationship, Solomon reminds him that values change with the times: "People don't live like this no more. This stuff is from another world. So I'm trying to give you a modern viewpoint. Because the price of used furniture is nothing but a viewpoint." The viewpoint each brother has of the other is not up-to-date; it remains with "another world," that of the past.

The very solidity of the furniture, an asset in earlier times, like earlier values, is out of place today, says Solomon: "the average person he'll take one look, it'll make him very nervous. . . . because he knows it's never gonna break." He bangs on the library table to prove his point. "A man sits down to such a table, he knows not only he's married, he's got to stay married—there is no more possibilities."

At the age of eighty-nine Solomon is reluctant to buy, delaying his offer of a price for such a large quantity of furniture that to sell might take more years than are left to him. He came hoping for "a couple nice pieces." To sell all the furniture "could take a year, year and a half. For me that's a big bet." He confesses, "The trouble is I love to work." Even while delaying, he is carefully examining the furniture, revealing his expertise, eating to keep up his energy. He consumes a hard-boiled egg and a "Hershey's" bar, relates incidents from his long life, philosophizes, and pretends to leave at one point when Victor loses his patience: "No, I don't need it," reminding him, "And don't forget it—I never gave you a price."

Finally, as Victor is about to dismiss him, Solomon decides: "I'm going to buy it! [*He has shocked himself and glances around at the towering masses of furniture.*] I mean I'll. . . . I'll have to live, that's all, I'll make up my mind! I'll buy it." As he moves from piece to piece, taking notes and making estimates, relics of the affluent past appear: a lap robe, a top hat, evening gowns. "And from all this he could go so broke?" asks Solomon. "And he couldn't make a comeback?" "Well, some men don't bounce, you know," Victor replies. With his zest for life Solomon is the opposite of the elder Franz, who after the crash was confined to the armchair: "Listen, I can tell you bounces. I went busted 1932; then 1923 they also knocked me out; the panic of 1904,

THE PRICE

1898 . . . but to lay down like *that.*" Like the furniture, Solomon was strong in his day. As an acrobat, he was "the one on the bottom," in a vaudeville act, The Five Solomons, "maybe fifty theaters." He left Russia at the age of twenty-four: "I was a horse them days . . . nothing ever stopped me. Only life."

While the crash, their parents' deaths, and their estrangement have darkened the lives of Victor and Walter, Solomon's reminiscences of his daughter are a reminder that family tragedy is not uncommon. Bit by bit, almost as a leitmotif, he alludes to his daughter. First, he likens Victor to her in his cynicism: "You're worse than my daughter! Nothing in the world you believe, nothing you respect—how can you live?" Toward the end of act 1, Solomon confides that his daughter, who "took her own life, a suicide" in 1916, "very beautiful, a lovely face, with large eyes," has been appearing to him nightly: "I lay down to go to sleep, so she sits there. And you can't help it, you ask yourself— what happened? What *happened?* Maybe I could have said something to her . . . Maybe I *did* say something . . . it's all . . ."

While the brothers cling to their illusions—Victor that he was self-sacrificing and his brother selfish, Walter that he chose self-preservation and his brother self-deception—Solomon is a realist. He accepts that "time . . . is a terrible thing," that change is inevitable. He knows with the wisdom of his years that the inexplicable must be accepted. Near the end of the play he mentions his daughter for a third time: "Every night I lay down to sleep, she's sitting there. I see her clear like I see you. But if it was a miracle and she came to life, what would I say to her?" Although he respects Walter, Solomon is not above offering him advice, suggesting that the tax deduction may be disallowed, and defending Victor when he accepts a price disparaged by Esther and Walter.

In the verbal warring of the brothers in act 2, Esther plays an important role. As Alan Downer notes, Esther is "the tritagonist; because of her the play remains a drama and never descends to debate."[5] Although she and Victor often disagree, there is understanding between them, in contrast to Walter and his ex-wife. Esther rightly suspects that Victor will, rather than bargain, accept a price that may be too low. Now that their son is away at college on a scholarship, she is tired of scrimping and claims that they deserve all of the money; she is infuriated at Victor's insistence that Walter receive half and relieved when Walter offers it all to Victor. Their reactions are in direct contrast when she and Victor learn from Walter that the father easily could have supported himself as well as paid Victor's tuition. Victor says, "The man was a beaten dog . . . how do you demand his last buck—?" But Esther boils over at this: "It was all an act! Beaten dog! He was a calculating liar! And in your heart you knew it!" She realizes, "No wonder it all seemed like a dream to me—it *was;* a goddamned nightmare."

Esther has another important function in the play: it is she who reveals, for Victor is too proud of his choice, the reality of their married life and the price she paid: "We lived like mice." She describes their own furniture as "worn and shabby and tasteless. And I have good taste!" She sums up their life together: "It's that everything was always temporary with us. It's like we were never anything, we were always about-to-be."

Seeing an opportunity to gain thousands (Walter's offer of the tax-deduction saving), she is at the end of her patience with

THE PRICE

Victor and gives him an ultimatum: "You can't go on blaming everything on him or the system or God knows what else! You're free and you can't make a move, Victor, and that's what's driving me crazy! . . . You take this money! Or I'm washed up." Walter's reentry saves Victor from replying.

At the end it is Esther who speaks a requiem for their lost opportunities:

> I was nineteen years old when I first walked up those stairs—if that's believable. And he had a brother who was the cleverest, most wonderful young doctor . . . in the world. As he'd be soon. Somehow, some way. . . . And a rather sweet, inoffensive gentleman, always waiting for the news to come on. . . . And next week, men we never saw or heard of will come and smash it all apart and take it all away. So many times I thought—the one thing he wanted most was to talk to his brother, and that uf they could—But he's come and he's gone. And I still feel it—isn't that terrible? It always seems to me that one little step more and some crazy kind of forgiveness will come and lift up everyone.

Strengthened by the encounter, Esther and Victor go off to the movie. She indicates that he need not change into his civilian suit, says good-bye to Solomon, and "walks out with her life." Victor puts on his policeman's jacket and tells Solomon that he will return for the fencing foil, masks, and gauntlets. While Walter has thrown at him the dress representing their mother, Victor has accepted their past family life.

In discussing the language of theater, Miller notes, "my own tendency has been to shift styles according to the nature of my subject."[6] In *The Price* the speech of Esther, Victor, and Walter is sharp and precise; it sounds realistic but actually is heightened. The language Miller invents for Solomon, however, is distinctively his and like that of no other character in the canon. With Russian-Yiddish idiom as its basis, his dialogue is in turn humorous, aphoristic, and ironic, while at the same time it reveals a personality as original as his mode of expression. His accent and his age set him apart from Walter and Victor. His years earn their respect and his advice their attention; their attitude subtly influences that of the audience. It is as if Miller were bringing on an Old Testament prophet in the guise of a Yiddish vaudeville acrobat, Solomon's former profession.

His lively observations are made memorable by their idiomatic flavor, which Miller achieves through displaced syntax, non sequiturs, and unlikely metaphors. Verb tenses are random: "I never dealed with a policeman." Adjectives and adverbs are reversed; metaphors are outlandish: "Anything Spanish Jacobean you'll sell quicker a case of tuberculosis." Aphorisms are askew: "In a day they didn't build Rome."

Typical of Miller's artistry, every element of the play has its purpose: structure, language, and symbolism support characterization and theme. Not a word is wasted; as Gerald Weales notes, "talk is both tool and subject."[7] In the first act interest is aroused immediately by the unusual sight at curtain rise: furniture piled high. Suspense is built by the occasion—waiting for the offer of a price—by the tension between Esther and Victor and by the arrival of Walter, which shatters the consummation of a deal.

The conflict between Walter and Victor approaches a climax as act 2 progresses. It begins with Walter's dissatisfaction with the price offered; Esther sides with Walter; Victor resents her implication that he is "an incompetent." When Walter suggests that the furniture become his tax-saving donation, Victor hesitates; he suspects Walter's motives. Now each successive speech reveals more of the past and upsets present assumptions. Finally, Miller eschews a pat ending; the brothers are unable to put the past behind them and to resume their boyhood friendship and trust.

The deceptively realistic dialogue and action, carefully and artistically contrived by Miller, led to some critics' dissatisfaction when the play opened in 1968. As Weales notes, however, "given an attic full of symbolic furniture and a life figure that is also a Yiddish comedy turn, the play is reasonably divorced from the realism that many commentators read into it and found wanting."[8] Another daily reviewer complained that nothing was changed during the action, to which Alan Downer replies, referring to one of Solomon's lines, "What changed, of course, was the viewpoint . . . as the audience was drawn first to one character, then to the other; the result was one of the rarest of dramatic (or human) experiences, understanding, sympathy, with all."[9]

Verbal metaphors reinforce the action and characterization. It was Victor's walk to Bryant Park which led to his deciding to become a policeman walking the beat to support his father; now, he says, looking back at his life, "all I can see is a long, brainless walk in the street." His decision caused deprivation described in images that evoke the life they led: they ate "garbage" and lived "like mice," "lying away our existence," charges Esther, "down the sewer." Many images are drawn from the household. Urging Victor to reach a decision on retirement, Esther says: "It's like pushing against a door for twenty-five years and suddenly it opens . . . and we stand there." Victor responds angrily to Walter's offer of a job: "You can't walk in with one splash and wash out twenty-eight years."

Often both past and present seem dreamlike. Recalling his past, Solomon tells Victor: "I pushed, I pulled, I struggled in six different countries. . . . It's like now I'm sitting here talking to you and I tell you it's a dream, it's a dream!" Esther describes the unreality of Victor's donning his first uniform as "a masquerade"; years later he is "walking around like a zombie ever since the retirement came up." Walter views overassessing the furniture for a tax credit as a "dream world." To Esther the misery of their pennypinching married life is both dream and nightmare; she concludes: "I knew it was all unreal, I knew it and I let it go by. Well, I can't any more."

Paying the price for past actions is referred to by both brothers, reminders of the wider implications of the play's theme. Walter describes his profession as a "strange business" with "too much to learn and far too little time to learn it. And there's a price you have to pay for that. . . . there's simply no time for people." Offered an administrative job at Walter's hospital, Victor suspects a payoff because he is unqualified: "There's a price people pay. I've paid it." As Neil Carson observes: "there is no external arbiter of moral values. Each man must set his own price on his actions and then learn to accept his evaluation."[10]

The furniture and objects symbolize the past and the brothers' clothing the present. Early in the first act Esther refuses to be seen with Victor in his uniform ("Why must everybody know your salary?"). Yet the uniform also implies law and order; a person wearing it might well sacrifice his life for another, as Victor has done. Walter's camel hair coat and general air of well-being imply success and evoke respect. Victor recalls to Solomon, "the few times he'd come around, the expression on the old man's face—you'd think God walked in. The respect, you know what I mean? The respect!" Solomon replies, "Well, sure, he had the power." The affluence of their boyhood is suggested by their father's top hat and their mother's evening gowns.

While the armchair center stage (in which Solomon seats himself) represents the fallen father, who confined himself therein, the harp recalls the mother. Walter offers it to Victor, who, "with a certain guilt," declines: "nobody plays." Victor was clearly his mother's favorite, as Walter points out with some envy, noting that it was she who bought the gauntlets for Victor in Paris, telling Esther that "she adored him" and that "by the time he could light a match he was already Louis Pasteur." As boys, the brothers shared an interest in science; Victor recalls that the attic setting was once their laboratory, where they would work harmoniously at night, the room filled with music from their mother's harp in the library below. Both acts end with Solomon counting out the money, the price paid for the furniture, into Victor's hand, symbolizing that the present pays a price for the past.

Having purchased the furniture, Solomon is left alone on the stage. He goes over to the phonograph and plays a record, the same one heard at the beginning before any spoken dialogue, "a Laughing Record, two men trying unsuccessfully to get out a whole sentence through their wild hysteria." Just as Victor had joined in the laughing earlier, so Solomon does now, as the curtain descends slowly.

Writing of *The Price,* Miller states: "In the militancy of the sixties . . . I saw the seeds of a coming new disillusionment. Once again we were looking almost completely outside ourselves for salvation from ourselves. . . . the play and life seemed to be telling me that we were doomed to perpetuate our illusions because truth was too costly to face. At the end of the play Gregory Solomon . . . finds an old laughing record and, listening to it, starts laughing uncontrollably, nostalgically, brutally, having come closest to acceptance rather than denial of the deforming betrayals of time."[11]

Notes

1. Gerald Weales, "All about Talk: Arthur Miller's *The Price,"* in *Arthur Miller: New Perspectives,* ed. Robert A. Martin (Englewood Cliffs, N.J.: Prentice-Hall, 1982), 189.

2. Miller reports similar post-crash behavior by the father of a friend, Sidney, at whose tiny apartment Miller claimed residence to be eligible for a job with the Work Projects Administration. Sidney, who becomes a policeman, confesses "that in his total refusal to compromise with the duplicities of business he had betrayed himself into another position that was just as false and inauthentic" (*Timebends* [New York: Grove Press, 1987], 245–47, 250).

3. *Arthur Miller and Company,* ed. Christopher Bigsby (London: Methuen Drama, 1990), 161–62.

4. Miller, *Timebends,* 542.

5. Alan S. Downer, "Review of *The Price,*" in *Critical Essays on Arthur Miller,* ed. James J. Martine (Boston: G. K. Hall, 1979), 157.

6. Arthur Miller, "About Theater Language," *The Last Yankee: With a New Essay* (New York: Penguin Books, 1993), 91.

7. Weales, "All about Talk," in *Arthur Miller*, ed. Martin, 190.

8. Ibid, 191 n. 3.

9. Downer, "Review of *The Price,*" in *Critical Essays*, ed. Martine, l55.

10. Neil Carson, *Arthur Miller* (London: St. Martin's Press, 1982), 136.

11. Miller, *Timebends,* 542.

CHAPTER NINE

Plays of the 1980s

*Some Kind of Love Story, Elegy for a Lady,
I Can't Remember Anything, Clara,*
and *The Archbishop's Ceiling*

Had Arthur Miller's plays of the 1980s premiered as works by a beginning playwright, they would surely have met with praise rather than with complaints such as Frank Rich's "the answers [in *Danger: Memory!*] . . . are at best ambiguous—a moral gray area where once the author of *The Crucible* and *All My Sons* would have found clear-cut blacks and whites" (*New York Times,* 9 Februrary 1987). Yet the five works of this period are consistently dramatic, the dialogue sharp, and the styles and subjects varied. Because of the interest in these works by readers and by regional theaters, analyses are offered here as introductions to works deserving the attention they are increasingly earning.

In these five plays Miller writes of love, grief, aging, memory, betrayal, and illusion in relationships that are friendly, sexual, political, and familial, in plays that may take twenty minutes, ninety minutes, or two hours to perform. His subject, says Miller, determines his style, which he may shift from play to play, "in order to find speech that springs naturally out of the characters and their backgrounds."[1] *Elegy for a Lady* is dreamlike and illusory, *Some Kind of Love Story* is a detective story, *The Archbishop's Ceiling* a choreographed pattern of shifting dialogue and movement controlled by a mechanical device, and *I Can't Remember Anything* a realistic "slice of life." In mid-decade, as Miller reached seventy, he wrote *Timebends,* an autobiography that by its title reflects his enduring fascination with the kaleidoscopic changes wrought by time. The five new plays produced in the 1980s span the emotions from comedy to tragedy; their action (or nonaction) may center upon two characters in a dialectical exchange or upon the complex interplay of a group. Each work has implications beyond the situation depicted.

In l982 *2 by A. M.,* consisting of two one-acts, *Some Kind of Love Story* and *Elegy for a Lady,* was presented at the Long Wharf Theatre in New Haven, Connecticut, directed by Miller. As *Two-Way Mirror,* the title of their publication, the works premiered in London in 1989. An "Author's Note" declares that "in different ways both works are passionate voyages through the masks of illusion to an ultimate reality." The reality in *Some Kind of Love Story,* states Miller, is "social reality and the corruption of justice." The style is realism with a difference. The dialogue, characters, and plot may sound like Raymond Chandler, but should what seems evident be believed? As the only witness to a murder for which an innocent man has been jailed, Angela, a call girl, holds the key to its solution. Being "delusionary," she both "conceals and unveils" the facts in order to hold the attention of private detective O'Toole, once her lover.

In what Tim threatens will be their last interview in his quest for the truth, Angela assumes three of her multiple personalities: the tough but frightened hooker also becomes an eight-year-old girl and a well-bred lady. O'Toole suspects her fears are illusory, including her claim that cops in a "cruiser" are parked threateningly just outside the door. He has seen no such police car. But, as he is about to leave, he spots the cruiser.

During the encounter Angela reveals that she has known intimately three of the major figures in the case: the chief of detectives, the murdered drug dealer who supplied him, and the prosecutor, who at the trial obtained a verdict of guilty for an innocent bystander. In these associations Angela has witnessed police corruption, drug dealing, and perversion of justice—but her evidence may be unreliable. Miller describes her as both "dedicated to clearing an innocent man and possibly implicated in his having been condemned. She is part whore and part challenge to his [O'Toole's] moral commitment to justice, and of course the reviver of his moribund sexuality."[2] When O'Toole threatens to abandon the case, she reminds him, "I'm the only one alive who knows. There are names that'd knock your head off." She tantalizes him with the thought that "The whole criminal justice system could be picked up by the tail like a dead rat." In the 1990 film version starring Debra Winger, for which Miller wrote the screenplay, the wrongly accused man is freed, but the guilty go unpunished; *Everybody Wins* is its ironic title.

In both this play and *Elegy for a Lady,* says Miller, "the objective world grows dim and distant as reality seems to consist wholly or partly of what the characters' needs require it to be, leaving them with the anguish of having to make decisions that they know are based on illusion and the power of desire."[3]

Elegy for a Lady is about grief and love and aging, about hopelessness and hope. Its elegiac tone echoes the music Miller describes at the opening: "a fine, distant fragility, a simple theme, repeated—like unresolved grief." The two characters have no proper names; they are called Man and Proprietress. *Elegy,*

Miller notes, is "an attempt to write a play with multiple points of view—one for each of the characters, plus a third, that of the play . . . like the neutrality of experience itself."[4] The setting is dreamlike: a boutique without walls, its displays "suspended in space."

A well-dressed older man enters, asking of the Proprietress, "Can you help me?" He is seeking a gift for his dying lover. As he considers and then rejects various items, the story of his love affair unfolds. While he is describing the relationship from his point of view, he notices that the Proprietress is the same age and has the same coloring as that of the dying woman. They carefully avoided a commitment, he relates, for he is contentedly married. Yet his sensitivity to his thirty-year-old lover is apparent in the care with which he is choosing the gift. He rejects flowers as "funereal," books as "either too sad or too comical; I can't think of anything that won't increase the pain of it." The Man realizes that it was their "uncommitment" that makes it difficult for him to choose a gift.

From the beginning the Proprietress seems to voice the feelings of the loved one. She insists the illness may not be as bad as he believes, that there are cures. She explains that the sick woman may be avoiding the Man because she "finds it unbearable to be cheated of someone she loves." She tries to comfort him with the thought that "it may be a case of a woman who's simply terrified of an operation, that's all.—I'm that way." Miller notes that "at moments the Proprietress seems actually to be the dying lover herself. A play of shadows under the tree of death."[5]

The Proprietress suggests to the Man another aspect of the affair. They never spoke, he says, of "negative things." "You met only for pleasure," she says. "Yes," the Man replies. "But it was also that we both knew there was nowhere it could go. Not at my age. So things tend to float pretty much on the surface." The Proprietress observes that there is a point "when it begins to be an effort to keep it uncommitted. . . . to care and simultaneously not-care."

She seems to know his lover better than he does: "You carefully offered only your friendship" she reminds him. "Then you can't expect what you would have had if you'd committed yourself": "To be clung to now, to be worn out with weeping, to be staggered with your new loneliness, to be clarified with grief, washed with it, cleansed by a whole sorrow. A lover has to earn that satisfaction. If you couldn't bring yourself to share her life, you can't expect to share her dying."

Her observations lead to his recognition that "if she makes it . . . it would not be good for us—to have shared such agony. It won't cure age, nothing will—*That's* it." They kiss, and, embracing him, the Proprietress says, "She wants to make it stay exactly as it is . . . forever." He decides upon a gift—an antique watch. As he departs, neither of them knowing the other's name, "on each of their faces a grin spreads—of deep familiarity." The loved one may or may not live. What has died, and what the man is grieving for, he now realizes, is the affair.

Dennis Welland observes that the two one-acts as a pair give a "new twist" to Miller's "themes of guilt and responsibility, illusion and reality, and the human capacity for love and suffering that he has always made his own."[6] Christopher Bigsby compares *Elegy* to Harold Pinter's *Old Times,* in which "even memory seems insecure." When they address each other as the Man and the dying woman, "it is unclear as to whether these are roles which they are adopting for the occasion or whether they are the two figures in question. . . . Like Pinter's *Monologue* what we see may be no more than the projection of a single mind."[7]

First staged in 1987, *Danger: Memory!* consists of two one-act plays about time, *I Can't Remember Anything* and *Clara.* Miller notes that he became "more and more deeply absorbed by a kind of imploding of time—moments when a buried layer of experience suddenly surges upward to become the new surface of one's attention and flashes news from below."[8] The curtain-raiser is a gently humorous account with somber overtones, of an evening meal by two elderly friends, a man and a woman, in the living room–kitchen of the man's small country house.

Leo, a theoretical Marxist, and Leonora, a wealthy widow, speak of death matter-of-factly. He is making a sign consisting of the phone number of the hospital where she is to send his body for an autopsy. She doubts the hospital will find anything of interest in his donation. Leo reads the capitalist newspaper, he says, to keep up with their wrongdoing, works the crossword puzzle, and, as a retired engineer, is assisting a local bridge builder with his calculations. Leonora, on the other hand, is content to do very little, if anything. She eats with Leo every day and drives her car dangerously. Because she believes "this country is being ruined by greed, mendacity, and narrow-minded ignorance," she chooses to ignore present events and evades responsibility by insisting she cannot remember anything. Criticizing the present avoids recalling the happier past, which might be dangerous for the two, yet memory keeps slipping in though they try to avoid it. It is the birthday eve of Leonora and her dead husband, Frederick, Leo's best friend.

Chastised for his "goddamned hopefulness when there is no hope," Leo is asked for a "truthful opinion about [his] *life!*" He replies, "Well, the thing is, I figure I've done what I could do, more or less, and now I'm going back to being a chemical; all we are is a lot of talking nitrogen, you know." Leonora wishes to hear a record by her son's music group in Sri Lanka and wonders, "Didn't you and I dance once?" Leo recalls, "There must have been a couple hundred nights when I'd come over and just the three of us would play records, and Frederick and I would take turns dancing with you 'cause you'd never get tired."

To the music of a samba beat Leonora begins to dance: "She is remarkably nimble, taking little expert steps . . . and her sensuality provokes and embarrasses him." As she dances, "he struggles to his feet and, unable to move more than an inch at a time, he swings his shoulders instead, clapping his gnarled hands. And she faces him tauntingly, reddening with shyness and her flaunting emotions . . . and as the music explodes to its crescendo she falls into a chair, breathless, and he collapses into another and they both sit there laughing, trying to breathe." Leo comments, "Well that's sure as hell not Indian music. Maybe he decided to stop wasting his time and start playing human music." Leonora responds: "He does what is in him to do. Just like you. And everyone else. Until it all comes to an end." The incident creates a poignant contrast between youthful grace recalled and present awkwardness accepted.

She departs, as he cautions her to drive carefully and observes, "We could have a lot more interesting conversations if you'd stop saying you can't remember anything." "Or if you could occasionally learn to accept bad news?" she retorts. He reminds her to phone when she gets home, and the play ends with her call, as he pins to the wall above the phone the number to contact for his autopsy.

The humor of their remarks as they gently bicker lightens the shadow of death, which they acknowledge as imminent; the sign with the autopsy phone number is its symbol. Despite their differences, they admit their dependency, but Miller never allows sentimentality to intrude. He captures in a brief encounter the irritability, the frustrations, the disillusionment, and the pain of remembrance of old age, but at the same time he recognizes the hope, the dependence, and the caring.

Clara is the more complex of the two works, a character study of conscience-tormented Albert Kroll, thrust into a shocking situation in which he must recall "a buried layer of experience" as it "flashes news from below." The reviews were disappointing; Gordon Rogoff complained that "Miller is continually presenting shadowy events that haven't quite happened within imagery that makes no sense."[9] Miller responded that the critics failed to understand the main character or even the story.

The story is presented clearly and economically; as it unfolds, aspects of Kroll's character are revealed, and an incident reenacted from "buried experience" provides a moving, dramatic punch and resolution at the end. In a bloodied room in a New York City apartment Kroll has discovered his murdered daughter's body; he is lying on the floor in a state of shock as Detective Lieutenant Fine enters. The dramatic technique Miller explores is to "cast off absolutely every instrumentality of drama except the two essential voices of the interrogating detective and Kroll—

the voice of realism and the flesh against the immortal spirit that transcends gain and loss; the death-in-life, and the life-in-death."[10]

The action, with flashbacks, consists of Fine's duologue with Kroll to discover the name of the murderer, believed to be a Hispanic man released from a jail term served for killing a girlfriend. Clara, whose work was rehabilitation of former prisoners, was having an affair with him. Cynical, believing in nothing but "greed and race," Fine interrogates Kroll to discover the man's name, but it eludes him. Kroll suffers guilt for having instilled in Clara the idealism that made her vulnerable and also for having abandoned the high aims of his youth by working for a shady construction company.

To denote the way a buried memory "flashes news from below," Miller employs onstage flash bulbs of the police photographers to represent flashes from Kroll's memories of Clara, some of them enacted. As she converses with her father on a Christmas visit with her lover, Kroll attempts to voice his disapproval, but Clara defends the murder as "rage" and an "illusion." After the recalled incident, Kroll admits to Fine: "I guess I am a little ashamed of one thing. I didn't tell Clara how strongly I felt about this man."

By the end of Kroll's emotional journey through memory he has recognized truths he earlier denied, and he has reaffirmed a lost idealism. Ironically, it is not the hard-hitting probing of Fine but, rather, the playing of an old record of Kroll singing which enables him to recover not only the name of the suspect but, more important, his old faith in people. A choral version of "Shenandoah" is heard, with "Kroll's voice, young and strong," in solo. Kroll summons up from the past, and it is enacted onstage, a memory of Clara as an adoring young daughter, to whom he is relating a World War II experience in Biloxi, Mississippi, when he courageously saved the black men under his command from an angry lynch mob. Clara's pride in him restores his faith, and, as she moves back "toward the darkness," he cries: "Oh, be careful, darling . . . Oh, my wonderful Clara. [*Straightening, joyfully declaring.*] I am so proud of you! [*As she vanishes, his terrified, protesting outcry* . . .] Clara!" He calls out the remembered name of the suspect, Fine rushes away, the recording stops, and "Kroll stares into space, standing erect and calm now."

Music and memory combine to create the dramatic effect of Kroll's recognition and acceptance. As Miller notes, "Must he disown it [his earlier ideal], suffer guilt and remorse for having misled his child? Or, despite everything, confirm the validity of the ideal and his former trust in mankind, in effect keeping faith with the best in himself, accepting the tragedy of her sacrifice to what he once again sees was and is worth everything? The play ends on his affirmation; in her catastrophe he has rediscovered himself."[11]

Both of the one-acts in *Danger: Memory* effectively portray the pain of recollection, whether in the cantankerous relationship of two aged individuals who were once glamorous and sophisticated or in an experience such as Kroll's, of going into World War II with "youthful hopes" and "faith in people" only to lose the ideal later in life, which Miller views as "a slice of our historical experience over the past decades since World War II."[12] In the *Christian Science Monitor* of 11 February 1987 John Beaufort points out the contrasts between the plays' "two vastly differing sets of circumstances with equally contrasting moods. Whether smooth or rugged, the path down memory lane achieves its destination within the limits the playwright has set himself."

More conventional in its form, *The Archbishop's Ceiling,* a full-length play, had its beginnings in the 1970s, although its published version was not staged until 1985, by the Bristol (England) Old Vic and in the following year by the Royal Shakespeare Company in London. In the 1960s Miller had accepted the presidency of PEN, the international society of writers dedicated to freedom of expression, and in 1969 he had visited playwright Václav Havel and other writers in Prague, then under Soviet domination. Miller learned that, when painters discovered a listening device in Havel's chandelier, he jokingly delivered it to the local police as government property. "But the joke was unappreciated as the eavesdropping itself was undenied." Although the incident prompted the writing of *The Archbishop's Ceiling,* the theme has wider implications: in adapting one's life to the condition of being overheard, is there "some essence in man that is simply unadaptable, ultimate, immutable as the horizon"?[13] Miller notes that "we're all impersonators in a way. We are all impersonating something, including ourselves."[14]

Reviewing the Bristol production in the *Sunday Times* of 21 April 1985, John Peter observes that "Miller's real subject is authenticity. Who are we when we talk? And are we the same when we know someone is listening? . . . No other playwright has recalled so vividly for me that curious sensation, both humiliating and eerie, when one's perfectly ordinary conversation can feel as if it had been scripted by an uninspired scriptwriter."

The action takes place "some time ago" in "a capital in Europe" in "the sitting room in the former residence of the archbishop." The "early baroque" ceiling, which may contain a listening device, is decorated with a high relief of "the Four Winds, cheeks swelling, and cherubim, darkened unevenly by soot and age." The room, its contents "chaotic and sensuous," now houses Marcus, a state-approved writer and Maya, his mistress, upon whom American writer Adrian plans to base a character in his new novel. Central to the plot is the dissident writer Sigmund, who refuses to compromise himself with the government; the authorities have seized the only manuscript of his important new book. Sigmund, says Miller, "is clearly the most talented" of the writers, and he "has perhaps more than his share of cynicism and bitterness, narcissism and contempt for others. He is also choking with rage and love. In short, he is the most alive, something that by itself would fuel his refusal—or constitutional incapacity—to accept the state's arrogant treatment."[15]

As an American, Adrian is unable to understand Marcus and Maya and their tolerance of a repressive government: "Does it smooth them all out when they know they must all plug in or their lights go out, regardless of what they think or their personalities?" he asks her in the opening scene. He suspects not only that the ceiling is bugged but also that she and Marcus may be government agents, inviting writers to the room in order to be overheard. Attempting to help Sigmund, the forthright Adrian is ineffectual in this atmosphere and can only threaten to tell the story in the United States "from coast to coast, including Washington, D.C." Marcus's reply is to offer him a brandy. In danger of imminent arrest Sigmund says he will resist and produces a pistol as the first act ends.

News comes that the manuscript will be returned by the authorities. Adrian invites Sigmund to the United States, where his writings are admired and he will be safe. But he cannot leave; he needs the persecution to survive as a writer: "If you cannot hate, you cannot write," says Maya. "They are your theme, your life, your partner in this dance that cannot stop or you will die of silence!" Although his departure could be arranged, Sigmund decides: "I will never leave. Never."

As all the major characters are writers, they are in a sense consciously creating their dialogue for the listening device. The writers wonder "at what point are we talking to the ceiling and when are we talking to each other and when are we talking to both at the same time. How authentic can an individual be when power—the ear of power—is right in his room?" asked Miller in a 1987 British Broadcasting Corporation television interview. In the second act Sigmund explains that the way to elude power is to lie: "not exactly lying because we do not expect to deceive anyone; the professor lies to the student, the student to the professor—but each knows the other is lying. We must lie, it is our only freedom . . . like a serious play which no one really believes, but the technique is admirable. Our country is now a theatre, where no one is permitted to walk out and everyone is obliged to applaud."

The ceiling with its device is an obvious symbol; the characters glance at it from time to time, indicating their awareness of it. But the fact that Miller invests it with splendor, that it is a baroque ceiling with angels, and that, though now deteriorating, it was once part of an archbishop's abode suggests that the characters recognize in it a power beyond their influence, one that may dictate their speech and actions, "something akin to accounting for oneself to a god," Miller notes in his introduction: "After all, most ideas of God see Him as omnipresent, invisible, and condign in his judgments; the bug lacks only mercy and love to qualify, it is conscience shorn of moral distinctions."

With the collapse of the iron curtain and Václav Havel no longer a hunted playwright but by 1989 the president of Czechoslovakia, PEN's aim of individual freedom for European writers seemed to have been realized. But two years earlier Miller cautioned: "It is a play of shaded meanings and splintered implications, of double and triple repercussions not altogether unknown in the political rooms of Washington, Paris, and London. . . . We were all secretly talking to power, to the bugged ceiling of the mind . . . even unconsciously we had forgone the notion of a person totally free of deforming inner obeisances to power or shibboleth."[16]

Notes

1. Arthur Miller, "About Theater Language," *The Last Yankee: With a New Essay by the Author* (New York: Penguin Books, 1993), 91–92.

2. Arthur Miller, *Timebends* (New York: Grove Press, 1987), 590.

3. Ibid.

4. Ibid., 589.

5. Ibid., 590.

6. Dennis Welland, *Miller the Playwright* (London: Methuen Drama, 1985), 167.

7. Christopher Bigsby, *A Critical Introduction to Twentieth-Century American Drama: Tennessee Williams, Arthur Miller, Edward Albee* (Cambridge: Cambridge University Press, 1984), 2:240.

8. Miller, *Timebends,* 590.

9. Gordon Rogoff, "Treadmiller," *Village Voice,* 17 February 1987, 99.

10. Miller, *Timebends,* 591.

11. Ibid.

12. Ibid.

13. Arthur Miller, "Introduction," *The Archbishop's Ceiling* and *The American Clock* (New York: Grove Press, 1989), ix–x.

14. Arthur Miller, *Arthur Miller and Company,* ed. Christopher Bigsby (London: Methuen Drama, 1990), 163.

15. Miller, "Introduction," x.

16. Miller, *Timebends,* 573.

CHAPTER TEN

Plays of the 1990s

The Ride Down Mount Morgan, The Last Yankee,
and *Broken Glass*

In the first half of the decade of the 1990s Arthur Miller produced two outstanding new plays and one that was puzzling as well as a novella, *Homely Girl,* and screenplay of *The Crucible.* Each of the plays deals with marriage as its central situation, with implications that touch upon politics, society, and the question with which Miller began his playwrighting career half a century earlier: "how may a man make of the outside world a home?"

The Ride Down Mount Morgan opened in London's West End in October 1991 with an all-star cast: Tom Conti, Gemma Jones, and Clare Higgins. Miller's "Staging Note" in the published text sets the tone: "The play veers from the farcical to the tragic and back again and should be performed all-out in both directions as the situation demands, without attempting to mitigate the extremes." The farcical aspect of the play is its plot: a man married to two women in different cities is able to deceive both for ten years until a car accident on icy Mount Morgan lands him in the hospital. Both wives arrive at his bedside to confront him and each other. Although his behavior horrifies the two women, he maintains to the end that he has done nothing wrong. Critics and playgoers were bewildered if not repelled by a central character who is egotistical, materialistic, and deceitful. Three years later, when a member of the audience at Miller's "Platform" talk in August at London's Royal National Theatre asked what *The Ride Down Mount Morgan* was "about," he replied that "it's in direct succession with the rest of my work. It's basically about the problem of sincerity: if you convince yourself you're sincere, you can do anything."

Lyman Felt—and his name, like that of the philandering Senex of Roman comedy, is descriptive—is a man of the 1980s, the "me" decade. A wealthy insurance executive in his late fifties, he has every material advantage, including a luxurious apartment, high-powered cars, and a plane, but he is discontented with his wife. He complains to Theo in act 1 that he is bored with "your idealism and your unadmitted greed for wealth . . . your incurably Protestant cooking; your savoir-faire and your sexual inexperience; your sensible shoes and devoted motherhood; your intolerant former radicalism and stalwart love of country now." On a visit to his firm's upstate office he meets the dynamic young Leah, and they become lovers. When they learn of her pregnancy, to prevent her ending it, he marries her, as she demands, believing his lie that he has divorced Theo. Both his married daughter with Theo and his son with Leah adore him.

In act 2 lawyer Tom Wilson asks Lyman, "What do you want?"

LYMAN: What I always wanted; both of them.
TOM: Be serious . . .
LYMAN: I know those women and they still love me!

Tom has received a call from the chairman of the firm insisting on Lyman's resignation, at which he is outraged; although the chairman's philanderings are well-known, Tom points out that "he doesn't marry them":

LYMAN: In other words, what I really violated was the law of hypocrisy.
TOM: Unfortunately, that's the one that operates.
LYMAN: Yes. Well not with me, kid—what I wish I do!

Lyman's assertion that he is beyond the law may sound familiar to those who recall the economic and political scandals of the 1980s. *The Ride Down Mount Morgan,* says Miller, is "a completely political play." Lyman, he claims, "is the apotheosis of the individualist who has arrived at a point where the rest of the world has faded into insignificance." This type of character, he continues, isn't new: "It's just that Ronald Reagan gave it the imprimatur of society."[1]

Having achieved love, wealth, and fame, Lyman is assertive and charming; he is also lonely and frightened, especially of death. In an image in act 2 death is a tailor fitting a businessman for his last meeting: "You've got to stand there nobly and serene . . . and let death run his tape out your arms and around your belly and up your crotch until he's got you fitted for that last black suit. And I can't, I won't!"

Lyman's dead Armenian father enters from time to time trailing a long black shroud, a symbol of death, and attempting to envelop Lyman in it. Sometimes the father speaks, reprimanding and even beating the "young" Lyman. In this nonrealistic play other episodes are dreamlike as well. Although Lyman is immobilized in a cast, he leaves it upon the bed to enact past incidents, including his first meeting with Leah, a trip to Africa, where he stares down a threatening lion to the adulation of daughter Bessie, and a visit to New York City with the pregnant Leah, whom he leaves briefly for a sexual encounter with Theo.

In the final episode, with Theo, Leah, and Bessie present, the shade of the father successfully covers Lyman with the shroud, but he struggles and finally "flings off the shroud—all they see is that he has been thrashing about." His victory over death prompts him to recall, as he had been unable to do earlier, the circumstances of the accident: he wished to prevent the death of the affair with Leah. Confined to a motel by a blizzard, he attempts unsuccessfully to phone her, becomes suspicious, and decides to drive to her: "'Cause it had all died in me, Leah—this whole ten-year commute was just . . . ludicrous! I was a corpse buried in that room. . . . I thought if I walked in two, three in the morning out of a roaring blizzard like that . . . you'd be so amazed, you'd believe how I needed you . . . *and I would believe it too!* And maybe we'd really fall in love again."

When at the end he swears to the women, "I've never felt the love for you that's in me now," he is reminded by Bessie, "There are other people." The three leave him. Alone with Nurse Logan, Lyman holds onto her hand and turns on the charm: "I love your warmth, Logan. A woman's warmth is the last sacredness; you're a piece of the sun." Earlier she had told him of ice fishing with her husband and son. He now asks what they were talking about, and she relates that they discussed their new bargain shoes. The play closes with Lyman's wonder and envy at the comradeship of the little group on the ice, talking with delight about simple, everyday

anything and then spending money on banjo lessons." Patricia as finally acknowledged to herself, however, "I have to stop laming him."

Karen confides that she has been taking tap dancing lessons, inspired by a rented Astaire-Rogers movie. She hopes her husband will be bringing her requested tap shoes and costume, "but he probably forgot." He has remembered, and when the four are together he agrees, after some coaxing, to sing "Swanee River." In a magical moment as unusual as it is unexpected, Karen, in costume, dances. But the magic is short-lived, and the older pair go their separate ways.

Alone together, Patricia tells Leroy of her hope to return home. She has realized, she says, that it is best to "only look ahead a little bit." When she asks Leroy what he believes caused her depression, Leroy attributes it to her family: "They were so close, they were all over each other, and you all had this—you know—very high opinion of yourselves; each and every one of you was automatically going to go to the head of the line just because your name was Sorgenson. And life isn't that way, so you got sick." The metaphor is a reminder that competition was a way of life for her dead brothers. Patricia recalls that Leroy looks at the line as an individual, not a competitor: he once said he would always be at the head of the line, as he is "the only one on it." Patricia asks: "You do compete, don't you? You must, at least in your mind?" "Only with myself," he answers: "We're really all on a one-person line, Pat. I learned that in these years."

She confides that she has gone without her medication for twenty-one days but fears returning home: "I'm not too sure I could stand it, knowing that it's never going to . . . I mean, will it ever change any more?" Leroy responds: "You mean—is it

objects: "What a miracle everything is! Absolutely everything! . . . Imagine . . . three of them sitting out there together on that lake, talking about their shoes!"

The Last Yankee

In direct contrast to Lyman Felt is Leroy Hamilton in *The Last Yankee,* which opened concurrently in New York and London in 1993. Leroy is indeed "the last Yankee," for he clings to the founding fathers' beliefs in independence, tolerance, and hard work. Arthur Miller in this play returns to the theme that shattered audiences of *Death of a Salesman:* the destruction of the individual and the family by the false values of the marketplace. Hailed as "a miniature masterpiece" of only ninety minutes, without intermission, the play treats four characters whose every word and gesture is significant. The plot is simple. Two husbands, one in his forties, one in his sixties, meet in the waiting room of a state mental hospital and discuss their wives, who are suffering from depression. In the second scene the wives speak of their present and past lives. The husbands enter, and the four interact; the older couple are still in conflict, while the younger two struggle toward an understanding and, shakily optimistic, leave for home. So true to life are Miller's characters and so deep his compassion for them that the play leaves the audience hopeful and even exhilarated.

Besides symbolizing long-ago ideals now lost in the complexities of modern life, *Yankee* here has an additional meaning. In the small town where Leroy and his wife Patricia grew up, he as a descendent of Alexander Hamilton and she as the daughter of immigrants, *Yankee* was the immigrant Swedes' designation for the hated majority, who looked down on them as strong in the back but weak in the brain. But in their own circles the Swedes considered themselves superior. "No Yankee will ever be good enough for a Swedish girl," Pat's father had told Leroy before the wedding. They were attracted to each other, Pat confides to Karen, because "we were the handsomest pair in town." In the values by which she lives appearance and material success are all-important: "My brothers," she boasts, "the way they stood and walked . . . and their teeth!" Both were award-winning athletes. Asked the cause of their suicides, she replies: "Disappointment. We were all brought up expecting to be wonderful, and . . . [*breaks off with a shrug*] . . . just wasn't."

Meeting Leroy in the first scene, Karen's husband John Frick is cordial to the younger man "dressed in subdued Ivy League jacket and slacks and shined brogans." Frick is surprised to learn that he is conversing with a carpenter because Leroy looks "like a college man." Respect revives when Frick recognizes him from a newspaper article about his being descended from Alexander Hamilton. The fact that Leroy is unacquainted with other descendents is another surprise for Frick: "Some of them must be pretty big—Never even looked them up?" Leroy answers, "Nope." While Leroy is proud of being a carpenter and building a beautiful church altar, Frick tells him his lawyer father "should've taken you in hand." Unruffled, Leroy replies, "He didn't like the law either." But by the end of the scene he must defend his calling: "Should I be ashamed I'm a carpenter? I mean everybody's talking 'labor, labor,' how much labor's getting; well if it's so great to be labor how come nobody wants to be it?"

A prominent businessman with dealerships and automobiles, Frick judges people by their app pation, and connections. The American dream h him. He measures happiness in material term: success in life with wealth. When he carries the marketplace into his home, however, his marriage and he cannot understand why: "A woman with e could possible want. . . . Suddenly, out of no terrified!" he complains in the first scene. That Kare something immaterial, like consideration, does not until Patricia suggests to him in scene 2, "She' treasured, you see." Karen has even been fearful of a the night because Frick needs his sleep for appointm day; for vacations she accompanies her husband on fishing trips, although she says she hates dead anim sight of catfish makes [her] want to vomit." It was on catfish venture that she broke down.

The basis of Patricia's disappointment with Ler shares both Frick's marketplace values and his failu ciate the marriage partner as a "treasured" individua plains to Karen in their duologue in scene 2 that "absolutely refused to make any money, every one dren has had to work since they could practically names." (Yet their seven children, Leroy has infor have all helped run the house during their mother' sences while in the state institution.) Nor is she unawa marriage suffers when she downgrades him for makin money, riding in a nine-year-old secondhand car, o valuable tool collection to the museum, and "refusing

ever going to be 'wonderful.' . . . Well, no, I guess this is pretty much it; although to me it's already wonderful—I mean the kids, and there are some clear New England mornings when you want to drink the air and the sunshine." He reminds her of what keeps him sane: "You just have to love this world." The couple are clear-eyed about their chances of success, but they are willing to try; what has kept him going during the twenty years of her illness is, he says, the memory of her as "happy and loving." Miller provides no easy answers, but the fact that the couple kiss and that she teases him about the car and the banjo as they leave suggests that they, and the audience with them, are hopeful.

The Last Yankee was praised in both Britain and the United States. Richard Corliss wrote in *Time* magazine: "In the wonderful character of Patricia Hamilton, we hear a troubled soul having a chat with herself. . . . She seeks release from the ghosts of her golden youth. But wry or wistful, she speaks with the reckless lucidity of someone liberated from drugs and intoxicated by the impending peril of real life."[2]

John Peter, in England's *Sunday Times* of 31 January 1993, observed: "No other American playwright has written with such power and unrighteous, un-censorious understanding about marriage under stress: the constant need for independence and reassurance, domination and comfort; the hopeless, helpless, battered affection people can feel for someone close but unreachable; the need to speak and the fear of being either heard or unheard." The "half-optimistic ending," notes Peter, "rings both touching and true: it has been bought at a price. There is no rosy sunrise here, no glib, perky rebirth, only a sense of survival fleshed out by dogged hope and the burdensome, unbreakable bond called love."

Broken Glass

In 1994 *Broken Glass* opened to critical praise on both sides of the Atlantic. While it ran only two months on Broadway, it fared better in London. The presentation at the Royal National Theatre was moved the following year to the Duke of York in the West End, its run there followed by an extenisve countrywide tour. At his preopening "Platform Lecture" in the National's largest theater, Miller was applauded for over ten minutes by a cheering, record-breaking crowd.

"This is a story I have known and thought about for fifty years," explained Miller. In the thirties he had known a woman who had lost the power to walk, and the cause, not being physical, was never explained. "I thought about it a lot, and years and years later realized that it was a hysterical paralysis. . . . One day I saw the image of that woman sitting there unable to move, and nobody knowing why, and it seemed an exact image for the paralysis we all showed then in the face of Hitler. . . . But I haven't written it before because it always seemed to be part of the past. Until two years ago, when ethnic cleansing came into the news, and suddenly it became part of the present."[3]

The play is set in Brooklyn in 1938, but the title refers to Kristallnacht, the night of broken glass, when the Nazis in Berlin smashed the windows of Jewish shops and synagogues. "I've probably been influenced in selecting the theme by the recrudescence of anti-Semitism in this world, which is something that I wouldn't have believed," Miller told Jan Breslauer. "It always comes as a surprise, whenever it happens. It's 'well, that's over with; it's not going to happen anymore,' and suddenly, there it is again."[4] Sylvia Gellburg, a Jewish housewife in Brooklyn, is obsessed with the newspaper stories of Kristallnacht, and, when she suddenly loses the power of her legs, no physical cause can be found. Her husband, Phillip, consults a neighborhood doctor, Harry Hyman, who unravels the mystery of her hysterical paralysis and who influences her to change.

As Leroy in *The Last Yankee* is a contrast to Lyman of the previous *Mount Morgan,* so Sylvia in some ways is a continuation of Karen in *Yankee.* Both women have domineering husbands; their own wants are never considered, only those of their successful husbands, to whom the firm is more important than the family. With each woman her repression must become manifest in extreme behavior in order for anyone to hear her cry for help. Karen develops a depression so deep she is confined in an institution; Sylvia loses the use of her legs and is confined to a wheelchair. Both confinements are symbols of a repressed married life following a constrained childhood.

Despite their desperate conditions, both women change and grow, though Karen does so only tentatively. She takes up tap dancing, something of her own, albeit incongruous, through which she may express herself. Sylvia's change is at the core of *Broken Glass,* a play so complex in the manner in which it combines the political and the personal and so compassionate in its understanding of Sylvia and her husband that audiences are deeply moved. Sylvia is someone "everybody on the block loves," and she loves them in return, her sister Harriet relates to Hyman in scene 3: "All her life she did nothing but love everybody!" Sylvia had to look after her three younger sisters while other teenagers were enjoying themselves. As a head bookkeeper at twenty, Sylvia might have had a career, but Phillip does not allow her to return to work after the birth of their son. For twenty years they have had no sexual relations because of his impotence and her reluctance to "shame" him by consulting an expert. When she sought advice from her father, Phillip was outraged and refused to speak to her. A divorce had to be avoided, says Harriet, because "it would kill our mother, she worships Phillip, she'd never outlive it."

Instead of the active and valued business life, to which she was forbidden to return, Sylvia occupies herself with household chores. Son Jerome is now an army officer, a career choice made by Phillip. When she is confined to a wheelchair, her husband is puzzled that "it's like she's almost . . . I don't know . . . enjoying herself," he tells Hyman in the opening scene: "I have to do a lot of the cooking now, and tending to my laundry and so on . . . I even shop for groceries and the butcher . . . and change the sheets." Sylvia now spends her time listening to the radio and reading books and newspapers. The news about the Nazis' treatment of Jews in Germany evokes horror and fear in Sylvia, who insists that action must be taken to prevent the spread of such cruelty. Those around her are a microcosm of the world's attitude; they react with unconcern or disbelief. Some, like Phillip, believe the refugee German Jews are too "uppity"; most see the Nazis as an abberation in a society that would soon come to its senses—after all, Germany gave the world Beethoven and Goethe.

But Sylvia persists. Perhaps because she has been victimized by Phillip's persecution (though he is unaware of it as such), she is especially alarmed by these faraway events. "The center of my concentration," notes Miller, was "the mystery of how this social-political dilemma lodged in this woman's limbs, so to speak, reaching across 3,000 miles of water."[5] A news photo of old men forced to scrub the sidewalk preys on Sylvia's mind, she tells her sister in scene 2: "One of the old men in the paper was his [their grandfather's] spitting image, he had the same exact glasses with the wire frames. I can't get it out of my mind. On their knees on the sidewalk, two old men. And there's fifteen or twenty people standing in a circle laughing at them scrubbing with toothbrushes." When Harriet asks why the people would do such a thing, Sylvia, "angered," replies: "To humiliate them, to make fools of them!"

Her humiliation by Phillip is reflected in the dream she reports to Dr. Hyman in scene 8: everything is gray, like a newspaper photo. A crowd of Germans are chasing her, one of the men catches her, kisses her, and then mutilates her—"I think it's Phillip." Encourage by Hyman, she interprets: "Because Phillip . . . I mean . . . [*A little laugh*] . . . he sounds sometimes like he doesn't like Jews?"

One of Miller's most complex characters, Phillip Gellburg is a self-hating Jew who at times sounds anti-Semitic. Dr. Hyman's wife, Margaret, characterizes Phillip as a "miserable little pisser" and a "dictator." He is proud that his name is Gellburg, and not Goldberg. The men of the neighborhood avoid playing poker with Phillip, who is uptight, disapproving, disagreeable, and "prickly." At the same time, says Miller, the audience is "supposed to really feel for him," because "he's trying to be invulnerable." Does he know what he is doing to Sylvia? "He knows with one part of his mind; with the other part of his mind he's denying it. He wants desperately to change."[6]

By exploring the causes for his behavior, Miller creates sympathy for unpleasant, buttoned-up Phillip. His impotence, he tells Sylvia in scene 8, was a result of what he believed was her rejection when he refused to allow her to return to work: "You didn't want me to be the man here. And then, on top of that when you didn't want any more children . . . everything inside me just dried up." He says, "I tried a hundred times to talk to you, but I couldn't. I kept waiting for myself to change. Or you. And then we got to where it didn't seem to matter any more. So I left it that way. And I couldn't change anything any more."

Miller describes the play as "a tragedy."[7] The tragedy is the waste of a life, as middle-aged Sylvia, looking back at a barren relationship, laments to Phillip in scene 8: "What I did with my life! Out of ignorance. Out of not wanting to shame you in front of other people. A whole life. Gave it away like a couple of pennies—I took better care of my shoes." "Given the mores of that time and society, and her amenable personality, and the influence of her mother, she was not likely to take an independent route, so she turns against herself," Miller explains. "Her inability to walk is first of all a real event, but some real events do become metaphorical."[8]

In the same scene, as Sylvia speaks to Hyman of Phillip's impotence and his violence, she "lifts the newspaper" report of Kristallnacht and stands on her feet momentarily: "They are beating up little children! What if they kill those children!" She is able to stand briefly, notes Miller, due "partly to her anxiety, which rises to a peak because she feels nobody is going to do anything about the suffering in Germany." It is "the first time she is taking her life into her own hands." It also marks the turning point in her relationship with Phillip. She may have been a victim, like the Jews in Germany with whom she identifies, "but she is also a revolutionary," says Miller.[9] Finally, it is Sylvia who is giving the orders, not Phillip. When Phillip decides to replace Hyman as Sylvia's doctor, she insists, "I want *him*. . . . And I don't want to discuss it again!"

GELLBURG: Well, we'll see.
SYLVIA: We will not see!
GELLBURG: What's this tone of voice?
SYLVIA: . . . It's a Jewish woman's tone of voice!

In scene 11 she informs Phillip: "I keep thinking of how I used to be; remember my parents' house, how full of love it always was? Nobody was ever afraid of anything. But with us, Phillip, everything somehow got . . . dangerous. Whatever I wanted to do, whatever I wanted to say, I had to tiptoe around you. And it wasn't me."

Phillip's realization is less dramatic but more painful. Like Willy Loman, he has bought the American dream and is proud to head the mortgage department of the Brooklyn Guarantee and Trust (the name may be ironic) as the only Jew they employ. Their chairman is clearly anti-Semitic. A yachtsman who is almost a caricature of a capitalist, Mr. Case suspects that Phillip allowed a company rival to acquire a wanted property because they are both Jewish and "you people" always stick together. Phillip is so enraged at Case's impugning his loyalty that he insults his boss, is fired, and suffers a heart attack. He now sees, he tells Hyman in the final scene, that he was being used: "He goes sailing around on the ocean and meanwhile I'm foreclosing Brooklyn for them. That's what it boils down to. You got some lousy rotten job to do, get Gellburg, send in the Yid." (The forecloser of mortgages in the Depression was a villain particularly feared and hated.) "But to accuse me of double-crossing the *company!* That is absolutely unfair . . . it was like a hammer between the eyes."

As the catalyst who brings about the change in Sylvia and the realization in Phillip, Dr. Harry Hyman is a contrast to Phillip. Contented, happily married, aware of his attractiveness to women, athletic, laid-back, and likable, Hyman resembles a younger version of Charley in *Death of a Salesman* or Solomon in *The Price,* one who stands outside the conflict, advising and offering an objective (often humorous) point of view. In the last scene he informs the ill Gellburg that self-hate is "scaring her to death." Persecution, he explains, is not singular: "I have all kinds coming into my office and there's not one of them who one way or another is not persecuted. Yes. *Everybody's* persecuted. The poor by the rich, the rich by the poor, the black by the white, the white by the black, the men by the women, the women by the men, the Catholics by the Protestants, the Protestants by the Catholics—and of course all of them by the Jews."

But it is too late for Gellburg to change, although he vows to Sylvia as he is dying, "I tell you, if I live I have to try to change myself." Sylvia balances herself, rises to her feet, and "takes a faltering step toward her husband" as the play ends.

Broken Glass is rich in symbolism. Central is Sylvia's paralysis as a metaphor for the inability of the outside world to act in 1938 as the Nazi persecution of Jews accelerated. Images of birth and death, babies and funerals, symbolize Sylvia's rebirth and the death of the marriage between her and black-suited Phillip. Describing the play as a tragedy at his preopening lecture, Miller added, "with a lot of jokes." "Something you forget about

PLAYS OF THE 1990s

Mr. Miller is that he can write dialogue with the best of them: wonderfully vivid, funny, ironic and economical," observes Vincent Canby in the *New York Times* of 1 May 1994. "He doesn't waste words but, because he favors prosaic locutions, his gift for language is not often recognized." His debt to Odets's style, which Miller defines as "poetic realism,"[10] is nowhere so evident as in *Broken Glass.* The dialogue is a heightened New Yorkese, flavored with Yiddish locutions, non sequiturs, and rhetorical questions. When Hyman observes that Phillip almost sounds "like a Republican," Gellburg replies, "The Torah says a Jew has to be a Democrat?"

As capacity audience after audience has filled the theaters to see *Broken Glass,* their cheers and fervent applause confirmed John Peter's evaluation in England's *Sunday Times* of 14 August 1994: "Miller explores the painful bonds between personality, sexuality and maturity with a fearlessness, accuracy and compassion which have no equal in the theatre today. . . . This grand, harrowing play, deeply compassionate and darkly humorous, is one of the great creations of the American theatre."

As one of America's three greatest playwrights, along with Eugene O'Neill and Tennessee Williams, Arthur Miller, in 1995 in his eightieth year, published a new work of fiction, attended a sell-out birthday tribute at London's Royal National Theatre, and awaited the release of the film of *The Crucible.* That, like Willy Loman, he has continued to "feel kind of temporary" is evident from the closing page of his autobiography, in which he writes that at a town meeting his forty-year "temporary" stay in the Connecticut countryside makes him the oldest resident. The six thousand seedling pines he, his wife, and their friends planted twenty-five years earlier have become sixty-foot trees among which coyotes from the North can be seen wandering at dusk. "They see my light and pause, muzzles lifted, wondering who I am and what I am doing here in this cabin under my light. I am a mystery to them until they tire of it and move on, but the truth, the first truth, probably, is that we are all connected, watching one another. Even the trees."[11]

Notes

1. Janet Watts, "Interview: Arthur Miller," *New York Observer,* 18 November 1991, 21.

2. Richard Corliss, *Theater:* "Attention Must Be Paid," *Time*, 8 February 1993, 72.

3. Peter Lewis, "Headlines That Unlocked a 50-Year Story," *Sunday Telegraph* (London), 31 July 1994 Review, 6.

4. Jan Breslauer, "The Arthur Miller Method," *Los Angeles Times,* 19 June 1994, Calendar, 8.

5. Ibid., 9, 78.

6. Interview with the author, New York City, 13 May 1994.

7. Arthur Miller, "Platform," National Theatre, London, 3 August 1994.

8. Interview with the author, 13 May 1994.

9. Ibid.

10. Arthur Miller, "About Theater Language," *The Last Yankee: With a New Essay by the Author* (New York: Penguin Books, 1993), 79.

11. Miller, *Timebends,* 599.

BIBLIOGRAPHY

Primary Works

Collections of Plays

Arthur Miller's Collected Plays. Vol. 1. New York: Viking, 1957. London: Cresset, 1958.

The Portable Arthur Miller. Edited by Harold Clurman. New York: Viking, 1971.

Arthur Miller's Collected Plays. Vol. 2. New York: Viking, 1981. (Plays through 1980. Subsequent plays published singly.)

Plays

All My Sons. New York: Reynal and Hitchcock, 1947. In *Famous American Plays of the 1940s.* New York: Dell, 1967. Harmondsworth, U.K.: Penguin, 1961 (with *A View from the Bridge*).

Death of a Salesman. New York: Viking, 1949. London: Cresset, 1949.

The Crucible. New York: Viking, 1953. London: Cresset, 1956. In *The Crucible : Text and Criticism.* Edited by Gerald Weales. New York: Viking, 1971.

A View from the Bridge (with *A Memory of Two Mondays*). New York: Viking, 1955. (With *All My Sons.*) Harmondsworth, U.K.: Penguin, 1961.

A View from the Bridge: A Play in Two Acts. London: Cresset, 1957. New York: Viking, 1960.

BIBLIOGRAPHY

After the Fall. In *The Saturday Evening Post,* 1 February 1964, 32–58.

After the Fall. Final stage version. New York: Viking, 1964. London: Secker and Warburg, 1965.

Incident at Vichy. New York: Viking, 1965. London: Secker and Warburg, 1966. In *The Portable Arthur Miller.* Edited by Harold Clurman. New York: Viking, 1971.

The Price. New York: Viking, 1968. London: Secker and Warburg, 1968. In *The Portable Arthur Miller.* Edited by Harold Clurman. New York: Viking, 1971.

The Creation of the World and Other Business. New York: Viking, 1972.

The American Clock. London: Methuen, 1983.

The Archbishop's Ceiling. London: Methuen, 1984.

Two-Way Mirror: Some Kind of Love Story and *Elegy for a Lady.* London: Methuen, 1984.

Danger: Memory! Two plays: *I Can't Remember Anything; Clara.* London: Methuen, 1986. New York: Grove, 1987.

The American Clock and *The Archbishop's Ceiling.* New York: Grove, 1989.

The Golden Years (1940) and *The Man Who Had All the Luck.* (1944). London: Methuen, 1989.

The Ride Down Mount Morgan. London: Methuen, 1991. New York: Penguin, 1992.

The Last Yankee. London: Methuen, 1993. New York: Penguin, 1994.

Broken Glass. New York: Penguin, 1994. Rev. version. London: Methuen, 1994.

BIBLIOGRAPHY

Screenplays

Playing for Time. New York: Bantam, 1981. Stage version: London: Nick Hern, 1990.

Everybody Wins. New York: Grove, 1990.London: Methuen, 1990.

Fiction

Focus. New York: Reynal and Hitchcock, 1945. Harmondsworth, U.K.: Penguin, 1978.

Essays

"With Respect for Her Agony—but with Love." *Life*, 7 February 1964, 66.

The Theater Essays of Arthur Miller. Edited by Robert A. Martin. New York: Viking, 1978. 2d ed. London: Methuen, 1994. Required reading, includes the 1957 "Introduction."

Autobiography

Timebends. New York: Grove, 1987. London: Methuen, 1987.

Reportage

Situation Normal. New York: Reynal and Hitchcock, 1944.

"Salesman" in Beijing. New York: Viking, 1984. London: Methuen, 1984. Miller interprets the play for the Chinese cast—and the reader.

BIBLIOGRAPHY

Secondary Works

Bibliography

Hayashi, Tetsumaro. *An Index to Arthur Miller Criticism.* 2d ed. Metuchen, N.J.: Scarecrow, 1976.

Critical Studies: Books

Bigsby, Christopher. *A Critical Introduction to Twentieth-Century American Drama.* Vol. 2: *Tennessee Williams, Arthur Miller, Edward Albee.* Cambridge: Cambridge University, 1984. Detailed and penetrating study.

———, ed. *Arthur Miller and Company.* London: Methuen, 1990. Miller, actors, directors, and critics discuss his plays.

Bloom, Harold, ed. *Arthur Miller's "All My Sons": Modern Critical Interpretations.* New York: Chelsea House, 1988.

———, ed. *Willy Loman.* New York: Chelsea House, 1991.

Carson, Neil. *Arthur Miller.* New York: Grove, 1982. Exposition of works through the 1970s.

Evans, Richard I. *Psychology and Arthur Miller.* New York: Praeger, 1981. Filmed in 1969 and published from transcript in 1981. Valuable dialogue with Miller explaining his approach to the plays through *Vichy.*

Hogan, Robert. *Arthur Miller.* Minneapolis: University of Minnesota, 1964. Good introduction to Miller, with excellent analysis of *After the Fall.*

Jung, C. G. *The Undiscovered Self.* Trans. R. F. C. Hull. London: Routledge, 1958. Miller's theory of complicity may begin here.

BIBLIOGRAPHY

Kazan, Elia. *A Life.* New York: Knopf, 1988. Details the productions of Miller's plays directed by Kazan.

Martin, Robert A., ed. *Arthur Miller: New Perspectives.* Englewood Cliffs, N.J.: Prentice-Hall, 1982.

Martine, James J., ed. *Critical Essays on Arthur Miller.* Boston: Hall, 1979.

Moss, Leonard. *Arthur Miller.* New York: Twayne, 1967. Considers the plays through *Vichy.*

Murray, Edward. *Arthur Miller, Dramatist.* New York: Ungar, 1967. Useful scene-by-scene descriptions of earlier plays.

Nelson, Benjamin. *Arthur Miller.* London: Peter Owen, 1970. Reviews earlier plays.

Schlueter, June, ed. *Feminist Rereadings of Modern American Drama.* Rutherford, N.J.: Fairleigh Dickinson University, 1989. In-depth analysis of Miller's female characters.

Weales, Gerald, ed. *The Crucible: Text and Criticism.* New York: Viking, 1971. Exemplary edition includes primary material, analogues, and definitive essay by the editor.

Welland, Dennis. *Miller the Playwright.* London: Methuen, 1985. Good analyses, including later plays.

Zeineddine, Nada. *Because It Is My Name.* Devon, U.K.: Merlin, 1991. Imaginative and insightful approach to Miller.

Critical Studies: Articles and Chapters in Books

Alter, Iska. "Betrayal and Blessedness: Explorations of Feminine Power in *The Crucible, A View from the Bridge,* and *After the Fall.*" In *Feminist Rereadings of Modern American Drama.* Edited by June Schlueter, 116–45. Rutherford, N.J.: Fairleigh Dickinson, 1989.

BIBLIOGRAPHY

Breslauer, Jan. "The Arthur Miller Method." *Los Angeles Times,* 19 June 1994 Calendar, 8–9, 78–79.

Brustein, Robert. "Arthur Miller's *Mea Culpa,*" *New Republic* 150, 8 February 1964, 26–27.

Carlisle, Olga, and Rose Styron. "Arthur Miller: An Interview." In *The Theater Essays of Arthur Miller.* Edited by Robert A. Martin, 264–93. New York: Viking, 1978. Intelligent and thorough questions receive illuminating replies from Miller.

Centola, Stephen R. "Bad Faith and *All My Sons.*" In *Arthur Miller's "All My Sons": Modern Critical Interpretations.* Edited by Harold Bloom, 123–33. New York: Chelsea House, 1988.

Clurman, Harold. "The American Playwrights." *Lies like Truth.* New York: Macmillan, 1958. A major director and critic analyzes Miller's plays and their productions.

Corliss, Richard. "Attention Must Be Paid." *Time*, 8 February 1993, 72.

Curtis, Penelope. *"The Crucible."* In *The Crucible: Text and Criticism.* Edited by Gerald Weales, 255–71. New York: Viking, 1971.

Downer, Alan S. "Review of *The Price.*" In *Critical Essays on Arthur Miller.* Edited by James J. Martine, 155–57. Boston: Hall, 1979.

Gelb, Barbara. "Question: 'Am I My Brother's Keeper?'" *New York Times,* 29 November 1964, sec. 2, pp. 1, 3.

Greenfeld, Josh. "'Writing Plays Is Absolutely Senseless,' Arthur Miller Says, 'But I Love It. I Just Love It.'" *New York Times Magazine,* 13 February 1972, 16–17, 34–39.

Griffin, John, and Alice. "Arthur Miller Discusses *The Crucible. Theatre Arts* 37 (October 1953): 33–34.

BIBLIOGRAPHY

Gross, Barry. "*All My Sons* and the Larger Context." In *Critical Essays on Arthur Miller.* Edited by James J. Martine, 10–20. Boston: Hall, 1979.

Hale, John. "A Modest Enquiry into the Nature of Witchcraft." In *The Crucible:Text and Criticism.* Edited by Gerald Weales, 384–87. New York: Viking, 1971.

Hanscom, Leslie. "*After the Fall:* Arthur Miller's Return." *Newsweek,* 8 February 1964, 50–51.

Hawthorn, Jeremy. "Sales and Solidarity." In *Willy Loman.* Edited by Harold Bloom, 90–98. New York: Chelsea House, 1991.

Lewis, Peter. "Headlines That Unlocked a 50-Year Story." London *Sunday Telegraph,* 31 July 1994, Review, 6.

"Miller's Tales." The Talk of the Town. *New Yorker,* 4 April 1994, n.p.

Neill, Heather. "Leading Role." London *Times Educational Supplement,* 9 September 1994, 15.

Porter, Thomas E. "Acres of Diamonds: *Death of a Salesman.*" *Myth and Modern American Drama.* Detroit: Wayne State University, 1969. Important study of myths and drama sheds light on Willy Loman.

———. "The Mills of the Gods: Economics and Law in the Plays of Arthur Miller." In *Arthur Miller: New Perspectives.* Edited by Robert A. Martin, 75–96. Englewood Cliffs, N.J.: Prentice-Hall, 1982.

"Records of Salem Witchcraft." In *The Crucible: Text and Criticism.* Edited by Gerald Weales, 361–77. New York: Viking, 1971.

Rogoff, Gordon. "Treadmiller." *Village Voice,* 17 February 1987, 99.

BIBLIOGRAPHY

Schneider, Daniel E. "A Modern Playwright: A Study of Two Plays by Arthur Miller." *The Psychoanalyst and the Artist.* New York: International Universities, 1950. Fascinating psychoanalytical interpretation of *All My Sons* and *Death of a Salesman.*

Sievers, W. David. "Tennessee Williams and Arthur Miller." *Freud on Broadway.* New York: Cooper Square, 1955. Definitive study.

Spindler, Michael. "Consumer Man in Crisis: Arthur Miller's *Death of a Salesman."* *American Literature and Social Change.* London: Macmillan, 1983.

Stanton, Kay. "Women and the American Dream of *Death of a Salesman.* " In *Willy Loman.* Edited by Harold Bloom, 129–56. New York: Chelsea House, 1991.

Stanton, Stephen S. "Pessimism in *After the Fall.* " In *Arthur Miller: New Perspectives.* Edited by Robert A. Martin, 159–72. Englewood Cliffs, N.J.: Prentice-Hall, 1982.

Watts, Janet. "Interview: Arthur Miller." *New York Observer,* 18 November 1991, 21.

Weales, Gerald. "All about Talk: Arthur Miller's *The Price.* " In *Arthur Miller: New Perspectives.* Edited by Robert A. Martin, 188–99. Englewood Cliffs, N.J.: Prentice-Hall, 1982.

———. "Arthur Miller in the 1960s." In *Arthur Miller: New Perspectives.* Edited by Robert A. Martin, 97–105. Englewood Cliffs, N.J.: Prentice-Hall, 1982.

Welland, Dennis. "Two Early Plays." In *Arthur Miller's "All My Sons": Modern Critical Interpretations.* Edited by Harold Bloom, 91–99. New York: Chelsea House, 1988.

INDEX

INDEX

INDEX

INDEX

INDEX

Library of Congress Cataloging-in-Publication Data

Griffin, Alice, 1924–
  Understanding Arthur Miller / Alice Griffin.
    p.   cm. —(Understanding contemporary American literature)
  Includes bibliographical references and index.
  ISBN 1–57003–101–0
  1. Miller, Arthur, 1915– —Criticism and interpretation.
I. Title. II. Series.
PS3525.I5454Z686 1996
818'.5209—dc20   95–41776

DATE			
6-22-06			
2-23-09			

WITHDRAWN